I'm turning on my iMac, Now What?!™

by Chris Sandlund

SILVER
LINING
BOOKS

NEW YORK

introduction

"Yes, I know it's supposed to be easier to use than a
PC," my good friend Annie said with a sigh, "but let's face it, an
iMac is *still* a computer." The idea of figuring out how to
use it was so overwhelming that her iMac stayed in the
box for several weeks after its arrival. "Why are computers so...daunting?" she asked while looking
through a pile of computer books she'd just bought.
"And these books just make it worse. I mean, do I
really have to know what http:// means before I can
send an E-mail?" she asked, her eyes wide with disbelief. "I don't
know what a carburetor does, but I can drive a car just fine."

   Exactly. When it comes to using the computer, we believe less is
more. That's why we came up with **I'm Turning on my iMac, Now
What?!** There's no jargon, no excruciating techy details—think of
it as a driver's manual for your iMac. Author Chris Sandlund tells
you just what you need to know to start up, write a letter, get connected to the Web, and send an E-Mail. And for a little bonus, a
look at some of the cool-looking computer software out there.
That's it. We promise fun, painless understanding. So turn on your
iMac and see how easy it can be.

Barb Chintz
Editorial Director, the *Now What ?!*™ series

table of contents

Starting

1

With your iMac at hand, you are now a part of
the brave new world! Now what? Connecting it and
turning it on. Oh, yes, and learning how to use the
mouse and what all those little things on the screen do.
It's all here in the first chapter. So relax.
The brave new world is just a page away.

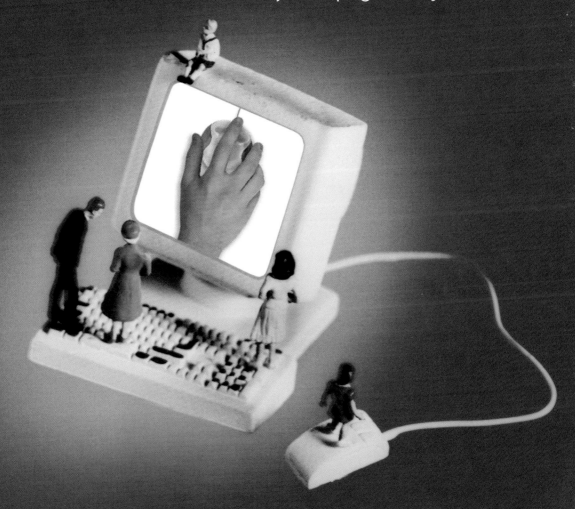

setting up

The computer arrived, and the box is sitting on the floor. Ready, set, go!

Chances are that you've just bought an iMac because a friend or family member told you it was easier to set up than a Windows PC. Despite their easy assurances, you may still be feeling a little anxious. Poking inside the box, you've found cables, manuals, and CDs (they're actually CD-ROMs, but that explanation's coming soon) that remind you of bad experiences with a stereo system.

Then again, maybe you bought it because you liked the idea of a blueberry- or orange-colored computer.

Regardless, you'll find that setting up your iMac and adding a printer is not too much different from connecting a VCR to your TV set. If your VCR is still flashing "12:00," this may still sound daunting. Relax. Get something to drink (preferably something nonalcoholic; you'll want to keep a clear head). To ease your concerns some more, make a call to the store where you bought the machine. Ask them if they have technical support in case you need help or if they can refer you to someone nearby who might help in an emergency. Or if they don't, see if there's a computer-savvy kid in your neighborhood who's willing to help.

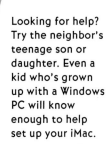

Looking for help?
Try the neighbor's
teenage son or
daughter. Even a
kid who's grown
up with a Windows
PC will know
enough to help
set up your iMac.

STEP BY STEP: UNPACKING

1. Unpack the cardboard box and lay all the contents on a table. You should have the **iMac** (the TV like device), **keyboard** (the plastic tray with the typewriter-like keys and a funny cord hanging off it), a **mouse** (the soap-sized plastic device that matches the color of your iMac and also has a cord). You'll also find **computer cables** (those plastic-covered cords, some of which have odd-looking plugs; others look like a telephone wire or the power cords of power tools), manuals, and computer disks called **CD-ROMs,** which look just like music CDs.

2. Save the cardboard boxes in your attic or basement in case you ever need to send something back.

3. If your computer came with a printer, wait until later to set it up. (See page 28.)

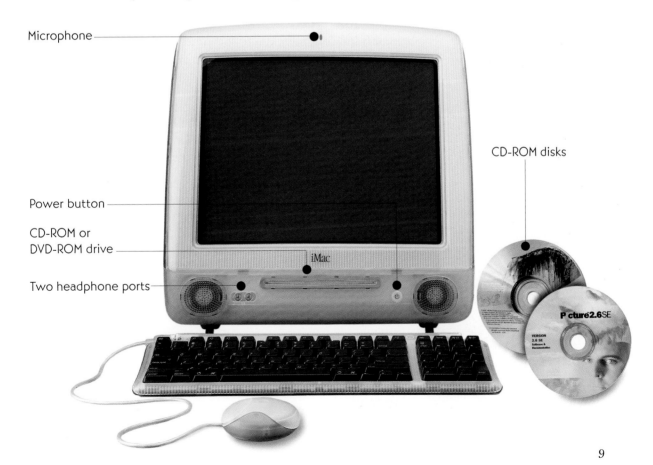

Microphone

CD-ROM disks

Power button

CD-ROM or
DVD-ROM drive

Two headphone ports

iMac

plugging in

*The parts
are sitting on
the table.
Now what?*

All right. You want to get going. This doesn't look too complicated. Here's a secret: It's not.

You should be able to hook up everything in less than 15 minutes—or 15 hours if you're really cautious. Get the instruction book that came with your iMac. Your goal is to hook all the items together with the computer cables. You'll connect your iMac to a power outlet and a phone extension. Now you'll plug the mouse to the keyboard and the keyboard to your iMac. (Notice, these cables have flat square ends; they are called **USB** cables.) Next, you'll plug the keyboard and phone line to some of the **ports** or openings on the side of your iMac, where you'll also plug in the phone wire. The power cord connects at the back of the iMac. See the following page to learn how to connect them all.

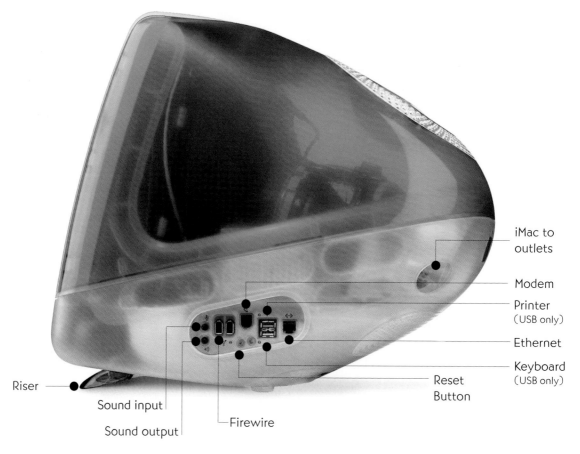

iMac to
outlets

Modem

Printer
(USB only)

Ethernet

Keyboard
(USB only)

Reset
Button

Riser

Sound input

Sound output

Firewire

STEP BY STEP: PLUGGING IN

1. First, if you want, extend the iMac's riser (the plastic bar located at the bottom of the iMac). The riser tilts the iMac up for easier viewing.

Next, connect:

2. Keyboard to the iMac

3. Mouse to the keyboard—on the right of the keyboard if you're right-handed or on the left side for lefties

4. Modem to a phone extension (more on page 58)
   Once you've made all those connections, find the standard electrical cables and plug those into an electrical wall outlet or a surge protector nearby.

5. iMac to outlet
   If you have a printer, wait and set it up later.

(more on page 58)

SURGE PROTECTORS

Surges in electrical power can be caused by a sudden drain on power, say, when air conditioners are in use, or simply due to a lightning storm. Surges can wreak havoc with the delicate insides of a computer, often ruining the entire machine. So it's a good idea to connect those computer cables that plug into an electrical outlet into a surge protector, then plug the surge protector into the wall outlet. You can get one at any local computer or office supply store for $15 or less.

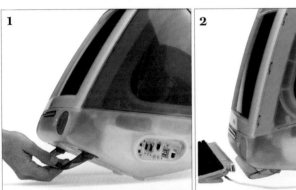

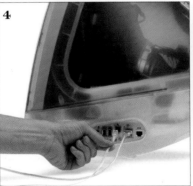

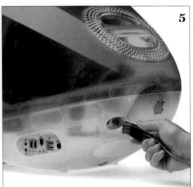

getting comfortable

The smart, ergonomic way to sit pretty

Is your iMac sitting on an old desk? A new computer workstation? A couple of sheets of plywood thrown across two filing cabinets? All those arrangements will work fine, as long as you've got a good chair. You'll save yourself a lot of back and wrist ache if your chair and keyboard tray allow you to do the following:

1. Keep your eyes level with the top of the monitor. If the monitor is too low, prop it up with some big books you never read. If it's too high, raise your chair or sit on pillows.

2. Have your arms bent in a 90 degree angle at the elbow when your hands are on the keyboard (without bending your wrists).

3. Place your feet flat on the ground without dangling. Better still, put your feet on a footrest under your desk to reduce lower back stress. If your legs are longer than the legs of your chair, make sure you can raise the seat of the chair or sit on pillows.

You will want a good lamp or overhead light to keep your eyes happy while looking at the monitor. If your computer is in a room with a large window, make sure that your desk is set up in such a way that you don't get that glare from the sun or you are looking at the monitor with the sun in the background. Each of these situations can make your eyes very tired and irritated.

HAT IF

You already have a good chair, and need a desk?

A card table will do if it's sturdy enough. Or pick up a second-hand desk at a thrift store. Or go all out and buy a computer desk with a built-in keyboard tray. All you need is a flat surface that has enough room to hold your monitor and keyboard.

You have the desk, but no chair?

Measure from the top of your monitor on the desk to the floor. This will give you a good idea of the proper eye level when sitting in the chair. Then buy a chair that puts your eyes at that level when sitting.

You have an overhead light and it's casting too much glare?

Kill the overhead light and put a lamp beside your computer monitor so the light is behind your computer screen. If that still doesn't do it, you can buy an antiglare filter at your local computer store. This filter fits right over your monitor screen, acting like sunglasses.

CARPAL TUNNEL SYNDROME

Most of us have heard of it, but you don't want to get it. This is a condition that is often caused by repetitive activities done with improper body mechanics, such as typing with your fingers above your wrists. Symptoms of carpal tunnel syndrome are numbness, tingling, or a sharp, shooting pain into your hand. To lessen your chances of having this problem when you are typing, make sure you keep your hands in a straight line with your forearms, not bent up or down. And try to give your hands frequent breaks.

turning it on

Let's get this show on the road

The keyboard and mouse are connected to your iMac, which is hooked up to the power supply and phone line. Now what?

Take a deep breath now. Go ahead and turn it on. You can turn on an iMac one of two ways. Either press the power button just above the F12 key on your keyboard or press the similarly marked button on the front of the iMac itself. You'll know immediately that you've done everything right when you hear a musical chord and then some whirring noises from the computer. This is called starting, or **booting up,** in techspeak.

You'll see a little square computer smiling at you on the monitor for a quick second and then a screen that says "Mac OS 9.0" with the phrase "Welcome to Mac OS" right under it. (Earlier iMacs say "Mac OS 8.6," while later ones have higher numbers.) That's because OS stands for **operating system**. It's the software that runs the most basic functions of your iMac. Once Mac OS is finished booting up, a cool little video starts playing to help you set up your iMac.

iMac
On/Off
switches

Don't Take It Personally

My husband gave me a computer for my birthday and I was thrilled, but also nervous about setting it up. The computer boxes sat in the guest room for the longest time. Finally, I got up the nerve and hooked it up like the instruction book said. Then I pushed the 'on' button and nothing happened. I unplugged everything and hooked it up again. Still nothing. Now I was getting upset. I called the computer store and asked them what to do. They asked if I was sure the outlet worked. Of course it worked. The clock was plugged into the same outlet and it was working. They told me to keep checking the wiring. I did. Nothing happened. I was sure it was me.

That evening my husband thought he'd give it a go and when he turned it on, it worked. What did he do differently? Nothing that I could see. Then it dawned on me, literally. He'd turned on the light switch when he entered the room. The light didn't go on, but the computer did... because I had plugged it into the top socket, which was controlled by the wall light switch. We've since plugged the computer into a different outlet and it's been working just fine. I've learned not to take anything a computer does personally. Just keep trying and eventually you'll find the answer.

Jesse K., Nyack, New York

WHAT IF

Your computer doesn't turn on?

Make sure that the power plug is securely attached to the computer and wall outlet. Also check the power outlet to make sure that it is working properly. (Do you need to turn on a light switch to power the outlet?) If the outlet is working, try unplugging everything and plugging it back in. Sometimes a loose cable connection will impede starting up.

Why is the square computer frowning instead of smiling at startup?

Because you've got a problem. The "sad Mac" indicates that something is wrong with your computer. Pack up everything and take or mail it back to the place you bought it. If this happens months or years from now, take the machine to a computer repair person.

logging on

*Computers like
to serve only
one master*

Great, you did it! You've turned on the computer. Now what? If this is the first time you are using your computer, it will want you to establish ownership. Fortunately, on the iMac this is relatively painless. In fact, you're probably halfway through a video presentation right now that will teach you certain elementary skills (such as mousing) and will collect information about you.

This first time out, your computer is asking you these questions to fill out an electronic registration form to register your hardware with Apple. (Your printer and any other extra hardware you've bought may have similar programs, only not as elaborate.) Don't worry. Your iMac is smart enough not to ask you these questions each time it starts up. You won't see the questions again.

It's a bit like filling out a warranty card, and there are often lots of marketing questions. What happens to this information? Nothing— it'll just stay in your computer. That is, until you get connected to the Internet (see Chapter 3). Then the registration information you just typed in will be **uploaded,** or sent to the computer hardware manufacturer, via the Internet. If you don't want to fill it out at all, click on the Cancel button, and it will go away.

STEP BY STEP: REGISTRATION

1. The video starts off by showing you how to use your mouse. Move it left or right, and the little arrow, or pointer, on the screen follows your command.

2. Next it will ask you to register your iMac. It's just like filling out a warranty card.

3-4. After you've finished answering all the questions, the video asks you whether you want to register now or later. Click No for now. This way the video won't walk you through going on the Internet. We'll cover going on the Internet in Chapter 3. By the way, your iMac will automatically submit your registration the first time you go on the Internet.

your iMac desktop

This blank screen with icons (or pictures) on it is called a desktop. Notice that all but two icons have names that are in italics. Icons without the italics are the actual items, such as the Macintosh HD (or hard drive) and Trash. Icons with italics are known as **aliases** and are shortcuts to the items. More on aliases later. Here, you should just note that they look a little different.

A Apple Menu: Click on the Apple icon to reveal a list of commands that will help you run your iMac. This is where you'll go to set up your printer and change settings like the date.

B Menus: Contains key menus, such as File, Edit, View, and Special Menus. Go to Special Menu when you need to empty the trash or shut down your iMac.

C Clock: Self-evident? Well, yes. But click on it, and it'll show you today's date.

D Application Menu: Click here, and you will see what software program or application is currently running.

E Application Aliases: These are shortcuts to several applications that play movies (QuickTime), let you browse Web pages, send and receive E-mail, find an item on your computer (Sherlock), and help you get on-line.

F Trash: Like a trash can under your desk, this holds items that you plan on throwing away.

G Control Strip: Holds shortcuts to several items that are also available via the Apple Menu. These include the ability to play CDs (that shiny disk to the right of the square computer), set up your printer (to the right of the check pattern), and set the volume of your speakers (two to the right of the printer).

What are those jelly-fish-things on the screen? If you have a blueberry colored iMac, the blue cyber-fish are standard for its desktop. Different-colored iMacs come with different desktop backgrounds. To change the color/design, see page 32.

18

using the mouse

Getting handy with your hands

The mouse operates best on a mouse pad, typically a 5- by 7-inch rubber pad. Naturally, a mouse pad does not come with your new computer, so you have to buy one at your local computer or stationery supply store. Do you really need one? Yes. The rubber pad lets the mouse move more easily. If you don't have a pad, okay. Your desk surface will do in a pinch.

The video that Apple provided to set up your iMac (previous page) showed you the basics of using your mouse, the soap-size device that serves to move you around your computer screen and to activate commands. But there's a world of difference between showing and doing. What now? Well, take another deep breath. It's a bit like a car's stick shift in that it puts your computer into gear. Ready to drive? Okay, start moving the mouse. See a black arrow? It's called the mouse pointer. Move the mouse up to the top of the mouse pad (a rubber pad that helps the mouse move smoothly), and the pointer moves toward the top of the screen. Move it toward the bottom, the pointer goes to the bottom. Right, right. Left, left.

The iMac's mouse has a single button. Press the button, and you'll **click** on whatever your pointer is over. Clicking is one of the most important skills you'll learn with your iMac. If you click twice in a row very quickly, it's called a **double-click**. Generally you click to **select** an item in your computer files, such as a letter, that you want to do something to, and double-click on something that you want to run (such as a computer program) or open (such as a document).

If you don't like the shape or feel of your mouse, several vendors now offer inexpensive covers that extend the body of iMac's mouse so that your hand can feel the direction in which it should be pointed. It's a small investment that will pay big dividends.

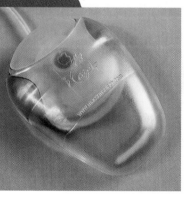

The round mouse can be cumbersome to use. You can buy a plastic oval adapter to fit over it at most computer stores.

ASK THE EXPERTS

What is an icon?

Any small picture with a one- or two-word name slug underneath it is called an icon. All kinds of things, from your hard drive or the trash where you throw away unwanted things, have icons.

How can I tell what each icon does?

See the bar across the top of your screen containing the words File, Edit, View, Special, Help? If you click on the word Help, you'll see a **menu** or list appear that includes an option called Show Balloons. Place your pointer over Show Balloons, and it will change color. Click on the Show Balloons option with your mouse button and then start moving the cursor over the icons. It will tell you what they do. If this feature gets too annoying, go back to the Help menu and click on Hide Balloons.

What happens when the name below the icon changes color?

If the icon's name is black, that just means you've clicked on it and selected it. If it's changed from black to some other color (generally light blue), press the **Esc** key, and the name reverts to black.

Like the steering wheel and gearshift of a car, the iMac's mouse gives you control over all aspects of your computer. When you move the mouse, the pointer moves around your iMac's screen. And when you click on the mouse's button, you are all but putting your computer in gear.

finding your way around

A quick tour through some of your iMac's basics

Before you start a journey, it's a good idea to know how you are going to get there. In the world of computers it's simple: You open and close windows. What are **windows**? When you double-click on an icon, a box appears on the screen. That box is called a window. The top of the box is called the **title bar,** which will have the same name as the icon. Now to close a window you simply move your mouse to the little open square in the upper left-hand corner of the window and click. You're back to where you started.

You can open up several windows at once, so you can flip back and forth between icons, software, or files (more on files later on). Try this experiment: Click on your Macintosh HD icon. A window will open displaying icons of all the stuff that's on your **Hard Drive** (or HD). Double-click on any of the icons you see listed, and another window will open on top of the one that is already open. (Each box opens like a window, hence the name.) To close, click once on its close box; keep clicking on each subsequent window close box until you are back to where you started. Congratulations! You've just traveled through the world of windows.

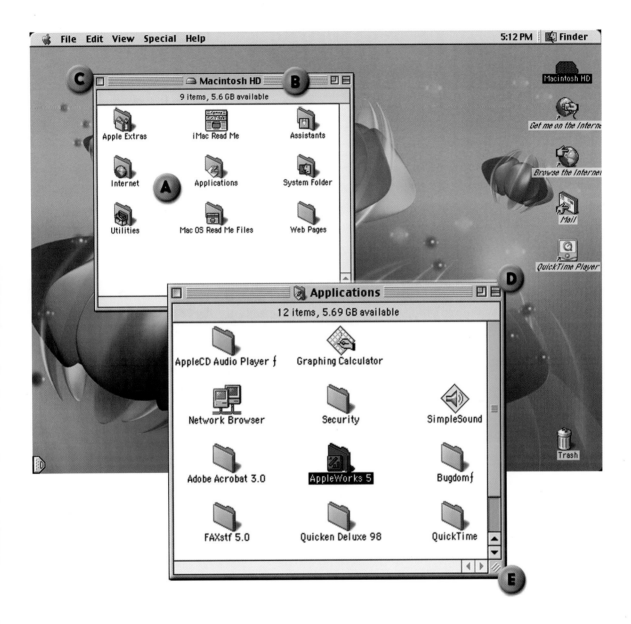

A Window – Displays contents of drives or folders

B Title Bar – Provides name of the window

C Close Box – Click here to close a window

D Minimize Box – Click here to shrink the window to the title bar

E Size Box – Click here and drag to shrink or increase the window size

loading it up

A little software goes a long, long way

Cooking requires ingredients, pots, pans, knives, a stove—the hardware of cooking, so to speak. But all this hardware won't feed you unless you have a recipe to guide you. Think of computer software as a recipe. It tells your iMac how to put things together the right way. Software comes in two main flavors. The **operating system** commands your iMac's hardware. It comes already installed in your iMac. Other software, called **application software** tells your iMac to perform specific tasks, such as word processing or using the Internet (more on those later).

When you buy a software package, for example, a computer game, or a piece of equipment, such as a printer or scanner, it comes with a CD-ROM—a shiny disk that looks like a music CD. These CD-ROMs contain information your computer will use to play a game or operate your printer. When you load them onto your iMac's hard drive, it will essentially copy the CD-ROM's information onto your hard drive.

Even really talented chefs rely on recipes to turn raw ingredients into a usable feast. That's just what software does. It puts all the ingredients together.

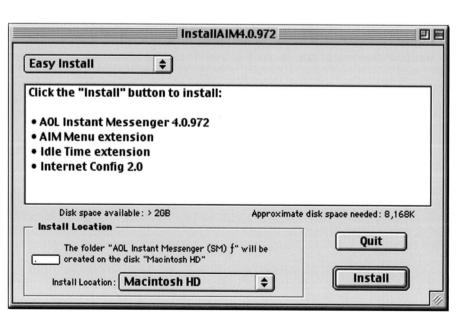

InstallAIM4.0.972

Easy Install

Click the "Install" button to install:

• AOL Instant Messenger 4.0.972
• AIM Menu extension
• Idle Time extension
• Internet Config 2.0

Disk space available : > 2GB   Approximate disk space needed: 8,168K

Install Location

The folder "AOL Instant Messenger (SM) ƒ" will be created on the disk "Macintosh HD"

Install Location : **Macintosh HD**

Quit

Install

You need to insert CD-ROMs into the CD-ROM drive by hand. Make sure the writing side is up. (One disk at a time.)

STEP BY STEP: LOADING SOFTWARE

1. Open the software package—usually a shrink-wrapped box. Find the CD-ROM inside.

2. Gently insert into the iMac opening. About halfway in, your iMac will grab it from you and insert it properly.

3. Your iMac will now make some noises, and after a while a window box will open and ask you if you want to install the software. Click Install. An **icon** (or picture) of the software will appear on your desktop. Double-click on it.

4. You will see some colorful graphics. Then it will **prompt** or ask you to provide a registration number. That number can usually be found somewhere on the CD-ROM plastic case holder or in the instruction booklet. (Without a registration number the software won't install. This cuts down on software piracy.)

5. Once your software is installed and you click OK, the software is automatically stored on your hard drive. To remove your CD-ROM disk, use your mouse and click on the CD-ROM icon and drag it to the Trash icon. That will immediately eject the disk.

6. What if the disk doesn't come out? Don't panic. This happens sometimes. See the tiny little hole next to the right side of the CD-ROM opening? Take a paper clip and pull back one end. Insert that end into the tiny hole and push gently. Your CD-ROM should pop out.

CD-ROM DRIVE

Inside the computer is something called the hard drive. It stores all your computer's operating software and your work. So how do other programs, such as games software, get in there? Through your CD-ROM drive which is built into your iMac. When you load software into it, the software is then **installed**, or copied, onto your hard drive.

The real reason people buy computers

Here's a terrific way to practice your mousing around skills—play come computer games. Luckily for you, one is already loaded onto your iMac; the other is on a CD-ROM, just waiting to be popped in and played.

Let's get started right now. If playing cards is your thing, try Eric's Solitaire Sampler. To find it, double-click on your Macintosh HD icon. Look for something called Applications folder. Open it, and you will see solitaire listed. Double-click on it.

If you'd prefer to see a more imaginative use of your iMac, insert the Bugdom CD that came with your machine into the CD-ROM drive (see the previous page for loading CD-ROMs). Go through all the steps to install it, but don't eject it. Bugdom is very typical of today's games. It comes on a CD-ROM because displaying all that scenery in so much detail requires a tremendous amount of **storage** (information), which would swamp your hard drive if you installed even a few games. So publishers typically distribute games on CDs, with only a small portion of each game going on your hard drive to read the information on the disk.

Once the software is installed, click on the Bugdom icon on your desktop. Watch as the world of bugs and ants and flies comes whizzing into view.

In the game Bugdom, you guide Rollie McFly around Bugdom's garden in his quest to free ladybugs.

setting up your printer

From your mind to the printed word

Most people buy a printer when they get an iMac.
Don't panic. Your printer came with detailed instructions. Get them out. Your goal is to connect this pretty simple piece of equipment. If you are connecting to an older, used printer, know that the iMac requires a printer with a USB cable (see page 10). Don't fret. You can buy a USB adapter (ask at your computer store) to allow your old printer to work with your iMac.
To set up your new printer:

1. Connect your printer to a power outlet

2. Connect the USB cable to the printer and your iMac

3. Turn on your printer

4. Now you have to tell your iMac how to use your printer. Go up to the Apple icon in the upper left corner and click. A menu list will come up. Select Chooser from the menu.

5. The Chooser window will appear with several icons of printers on the *left*. It may already have your printer listed. If so, just click on it. If not, click on one whose name is similar to your printer's. If necessary, choose USB under the "Select a printer port" option on the window's right side. You will see a listing of your printer in the *right*-hand side of the Chooser window. Click on Setup and then close the Chooser window. You will see a small printer icon appear on your desktop.

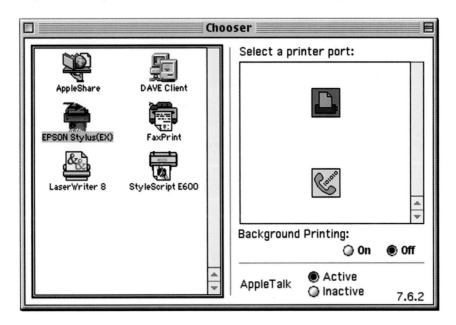

6. If you don't see your printer's icon, you'll need to insert the printer's software's CD-ROM into your CD-ROM drive. (See page 25 to load software.) Repeat step number 5 above. Once you've selected the printer, close the Chooser window, and you'll see a small Printer icon appear on your desktop.

7. To make sure everything's working correctly, click on the File menu at the top of your screen and select Print Desktop. The iMac should say that it's printing and then you should hear your printer make noises as it starts to print.

turning it off

Get me outta here

Okay. That's enough for one session. You did brilliantly. But enough is enough. Do you just want to turn off the machine? Go ahead. Try. Hit the power button on your keyboard (or the one on the front of your iMac).

Surprise! You see a window that asks, "Are you sure you want to shut down your computer now?" It provides four options: Restart, Sleep, Cancel, and Shut Down. Click on Shut Down. There's an important reason that Apple built this safeguard into the system. Computers prefer to turn themselves off in an orderly fashion. If you accidentally hit the power button and your iMac shut down without asking, all your work could be lost.

There's another way that Apple lets you turn off your iMac. Click on the Special menu, and you'll see the option Shut Down. (Also note that Special is where you go to Empty Trash, which is a good idea before you turn off the computer for the night.)

iMac
On/Off
switches

HAT IF

**You change your mind and decide you don't want to shut down the
iMac when you see the Shut Down window?**

Click on the Cancel option, and you'll be right back where you
were.

What does sleep mean?

If you click on Sleep, your monitor screen will go dark. However,
your computer is still running. Sleep is basically a way to extend
the life of your monitor by saving wear and tear on it.

There was a power outage when your iMac was on?

Don't worry. Restart your iMac and—assuming that nothing was
damaged by the electrical slump or that you have a surge protector—it will come back on with a stern reminder that you need to
turn off the computer with the Shut Down command.

Will your printer turn off when you turn off your iMac?

No. Because the iMac is a one-piece computer, shutting it down
turns off everything *except* your printer. Help conserve energy by
remembering to turn off your printer too.

now what do I do?

Answers to common problems

Do I have to turn the iMac off every time I finish working?

No. You can leave your computer on for hours, but it's generally a good idea to turn it off once a day. Note this: If you stop working on your iMac, after a while it will go to **sleep** (your screen will go blank). The minute you hit the spacebar, it will wake up your iMac and the screen will light up.

I spilled soda all over my keyboard. What can I do?

Use your mouse to shut down your iMac. Once everything is off, unplug the keyboard from the iMac and the mouse from the keyboard. Take the keyboard to a sink and turn it upside down to drain as much liquid as possible from the surface. Use a paper towel to clean off the keyboard. You can use a hair dryer or a cotton swab to dry moisture from under the keys. (Use water or denatured alcohol to clean the keys.) When it's dry, plug the keyboard back in, and everything should be fine.

The iMac just stopped working and froze the screen. What can I do?

Don't panic. This happens to all computers, even Macs. Computer techies call it **crashing**. Hold down the Apple key next to the space bar on your keyboard while also holding down the Option key and the Esc key. This should close down whatever it was that caused it to crash. Unfortunately, you'll lose any work that you had in progress. If that doesn't work, hold down the Apple and Option keys while simultaneously pressing the power button on your keyboard. If that doesn't do it, then push the **reset** button located on the side of your iMac. This will restart your iMac. A message will come up saying you closed your computer improperly. Don't fret. Just click Done, and you'll see your good old desktop again.

How do I change the color and design on my desktop?

Go up to the Apple and click on it. A list or **menu** apppears. While still holding down your mouse, select Control Panels. A second menu will come down, select Appearance. A box will open with tabs across its top. Click on the Desktop tab. Scroll through the various colors/designs. When you find the one you like, click Set Desktop and your desktop will magically change color. Close the box and your iMac desktop sports a new design.

I move my mouse but the pointer on the screen jumps around herky-jerky. What can I do?

Lint is probably caught in your mouse. Turn the mouse over. See the little round ball surrounded by a ribbed plastic collar. Press down gently and then turn the ribbed collar counterclockwise until the collar comes off. Now you can remove the mouse ball and wipe it clean. (You can also clean the side-rollers where the ball sits with cotton swabs and denatured alcohol.) Put the ball back in and screw its collar back on and it should work fine. If not, consider buying another mouse.

How do I change the date and time on my computer?

Apple sets the date at its factory before shipping a computer off. If you need to reset the time, click on the Apple menu and select Control Panels. You'll see a second menu, which contains an option for Date & Time. Click on this option, and the Date & Time window appears where—you guessed it—you can change the date and time. Once you've set the time, click on the close box, and the clock at the top of your screen will show the correct time.

 ELPFUL RESOURCES

CONTACTS	BOOKS
Apple Computer Corp. www.apple.com 1-800-692-7753	**The Little iMac Book** By Robin Williams
	The Macintosh Bible (7th Edition) By Sharon Zardetto Aker
Macsense Connectivity www.macsensetech.com 1-408-844-0320	**Sad Macs, Bombs, and Other Disasters: And What to Do About Them** By Ted Landau
	Mac Answers!: Certified Tech Support By Bob Levitus and Shelly Brisbin

Writing a letter

2

A computer's blank page is somehow less
daunting than a real piece of blank paper.
Maybe that's because it's so easy to fix your mistakes
on a computer. You can even change the tabs,
check for spelling errors, and select new fonts.
All these things and more you'll discover
in this chapter.

the blank page

*Compose words
on a page*

Every time you start up your word processing software (which you use to write), your computer presents you with a blank page. It's just waiting for you to start typing.

Here's how to open a blank page or document. Double-click on the Macintosh Hard Drive icon (the picture that looks like a little hut) on your desktop and then double-click on Applications. Then double-click on AppleWorks. AppleWorks is Apple's own software that allows you to do many things, including writing letters. Some people will try to convince you to buy a more popular word processing program, most notably Microsoft Word. These programs include more sophisticated features than AppleWorks. But AppleWorks does fine for writing letters.

Once you double-click on the AppleWorks icon, the program will start (also known as open or load in techspeak). The first time you run AppleWorks, it will ask you for your registration number—which you'll find on the package that contained all the CD-ROMs that came with your iMac. (These CD-ROMs are there for backup in case something goes wrong with your hard drive and you need to reload the software.) Type in the number, and it will tell you what to do next. When you are all set up, you will then be presented with a menu asking what type of document you want to create. Word processing should be selected already (if it isn't, just click on it) and then click on OK. You'll see a window called "untitled (WP)," under which lies a ruler, some icons, and what looks like a blank sheet of white paper. Notice the blinking line on the page? It is called a **cursor,** which marks where letters appear when you start typing. Move the mouse pointer over the rectangle on the page and it changes to an I-beam shape.

ASK THE EXPERTS

How do I get word processing software into my computer?

Apple already installed AppleWorks on your iMac before it left the factory. All you need to do is type in your registration number, which you'll find on the box containing the CD-ROMs that shipped with your computer. If you need to add another word processing program, such as Microsoft Word, first make sure you buy the right version of the software. You need the Mac OS version of a word processor, not the Windows version. Then follow the directions in Chapter 1's section called "Loading It Up," on page 25.

How do I turn off my word processing software?

Go up to the menu bar at the top of your screen and click on the word File. A short menu will drop down. Select Quit. Whatever window was open will automatically close. Before it does, it will ask you if you want to save. For now, click on No. (More on saving later in this chapter.)

QUICK LAUNCH

Hunting through your computer to launch Apple-Works can be time consuming. Here's a faster way to get started. Open your Macintosh HD by double-clicking on its icon. It will list all your software programs in the Applications folder. Find the AppleWorks icon and click on it once to select (but not launch) it. Next, click on the File menu and select the Make Alias option. You'll see a copy of the Application icon, but the icon's name is now in italics with the word "alias" added to the end. Drag this icon from the folder to the desktop. Next time you want to write a letter, just double-click on the alias.

37

the filled page

Clickety-clack, I wrote that!

You're all set to type. Go ahead, just start typing. Try a letter to a friend, letting her know that you just bought a computer and are learning how to use it. As you type the body of the letter, the words will start to approach the right-hand margin of the page. Keep typing. When it looks as if there's no more room, your words magically begin appearing on the next line. This feature is known as wrapping text and is one of many reasons that you'll never go back to a typewriter after learning how to use your word processor.

Another convenience is that you can change the **typeface,** or font, on your screen to make your work look the way you want. Each font has a name, such as Helvetica and Times Roman. Your word processing software automatically chooses a font for you, called the **default** font. Most word processors have several fonts for you to choose from (see page 46 to change your font). You can also select the size of the letters and numbers, measured in **points**. Generally, word processors set the size to 12 points by default. Size 10 works well, too, but is smaller—and harder to read—than 12. Larger point sizes are used for headlines or to call attention to a section.

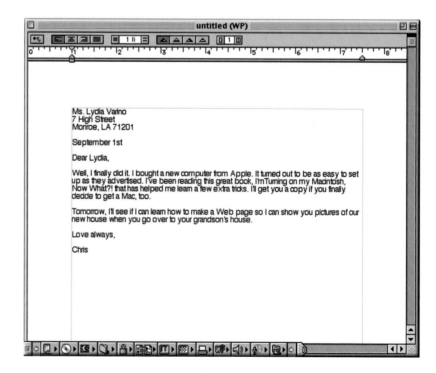

Now that you've got some text on the page, move your pointer over the middle of a paragraph so it becomes an I-beam and click to move the cursor to that spot. If you're in the middle of a word, you can move the cursor to the left or right (and up or down one line) by using the **directional keys**—the arrows that point in those directions—at the bottom right on the keyboard.

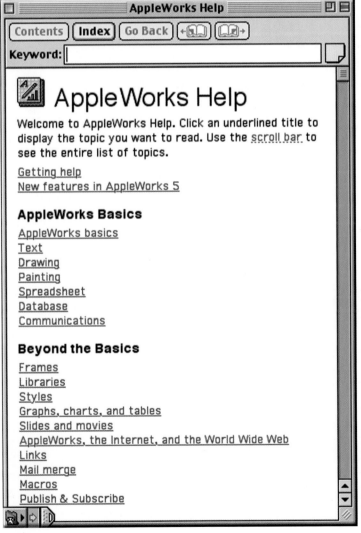

If you need help, go up to the Help menu at the top of your screen and click. Next, select AppleWorks Help Contents. A list of topics will appear (shown here). Click on the one you have questions about.

saving your work

The mysteries of files and folders explored

Until now the document has had the name "untitled (WP)" on the title bar. But in order to retain your letters for future use, you must always **save** your work. Saving means giving your document a name and cataloguing it somewhere in your computer. That means when you go to save your work, it will be saved as a **file** (a computer document that can be easily stored and retrieved). Files are then usually stored in **folders**. Think of a file as, say, your electric bill. After you've paid it, you put it in your paid bills folder. Your computer organizes your work in the same way.

How do you save a file? Click on the File menu and choose the Save option. You'll see a save window. The bar at the top says AppleWorks 5 with up and down arrows. This lets you know that you're in the AppleWorks 5 folder. You can replace the word "untitled" in the box at the bottom. Just type in a word or two that you prefer and click on the Save option on the right. It will place a copy of your letter on your hard drive, where you'll always find it.

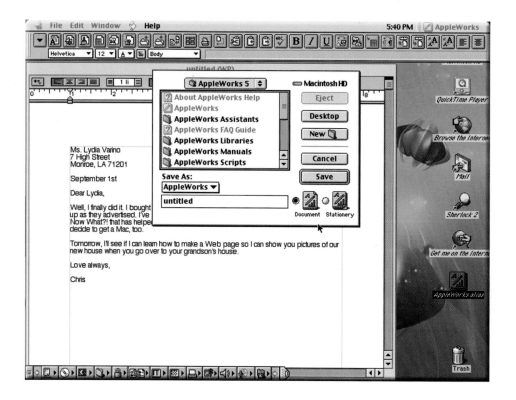

HAT IF

You want to save your letter to a particular folder?

When you hit the Save button, your file will be stored automatically to the last folder in which you stored something. (If this is your very first letter, it will be saved to the AppleWorks folder.) If you want to save it to a particular folder, you need to click on the Save As button. A window will open and ask you which folder in AppleWorks you'd like. Choose one, or if you wish, save it to your Desktop by clicking on Desktop. Or save it to a folder on your Macintosh hard drive.

You want to create a new folder?

Easy as pie. If you just opened up AppleWorks, simply go up to the File menu and click on New Folder. A window will open and it will prompt you to type in the name of the folder and then select where you want it stored.

If you are already working in AppleWorks—say you've got a letter on your screen right now—then go up to the Applications menu (far upper right-hand corner) where you see the name AppleWorks. Click on the name and choose Hide Appleworks. Your letter will disappear, and you will see your desktop. (You will also see an icon of a profile face where the name AppleWorks used to be.) Click on Macintosh HD. Now go up to the File menu and select New Folder. Type in the name you want for your folder and where you want it stored. Fine, you're doing great. Now go back up to the Applications menu and click on Finder—that funny profile icon. Select AppleWorks. Your letter will reappear. Now you can save it to the folder you just created.

You gave your file the wrong name. Can you change it?

Sure. You've got two choices. 1) Click on File and choose the Save As option. You'll see a window similar to the Save window, with the name highlighted. You can type in a new name right over the old one and then click Save. The file with the old name still exists. 2) If you've already closed the file, find where you've stored it and click once on its name, then type a new name. (The file with the old name is now permanently gone.)

editing your work

Don't like that
word—change it

If you've never had to use a typewriter, you don't know how lucky you are. When you wanted to add a paragraph (or worse, a sentence) to a letter or paper, you had to start over and retype entire pages. That's why a word processor is such a joy for anyone who learned to type on a typewriter. You can add sentences, move them around, delete them, or do any number of other things, such as change the margins or typeface.

To add words, you use your mouse pointer to place the word processor's **cursor** exactly where you want to make the change— remember that it turns into an I-beam over text to let you place it more accurately. Put it at the beginning of a word, a sentence, or a paragraph to type in a new one. To delete words, double-click on the offending word to **highlight** it (show it in reverse, white letters on black) and press the Delete key on your keyboard or click on the Cut icon just under the Window menu in AppleWorks. To delete whole sentences and paragraphs, double-click on the first word and hold down the mouse button while you drag over the section to highlight everything you want to cut. Then press Delete or click on the Cut icon.

Highlighting also lets you move a word, sentence, or paragraph. Place the pointer over the text you want to move, then click and hold down the mouse button. You can now drag the highlighted selection anywhere in the document.

The icon to the right of AppleWorks' Cut icon is called the **Copy** button. It makes a copy of any section that you've highlighted— without cutting it—and puts it in the **clipboard,** a place where the computer temporarily stores information that you have cut or copied to paste elsewhere. Place your cursor in another section of your text and click on the **Paste** button to put the cut or copied section in a new location.

STEP BY STEP: MOVING TEXT AROUND

1. To move a section of text, highlight it by double-clicking on the first word and holding down the mouse button while you drag over the selection.

2. Once a section is highlighted, click on the Cut button to remove it from its current spot.

3. With the text now gone, move the cursor to the spot where you want to place the text.

4. Click on the Paste button and the selection reappears in the new position.

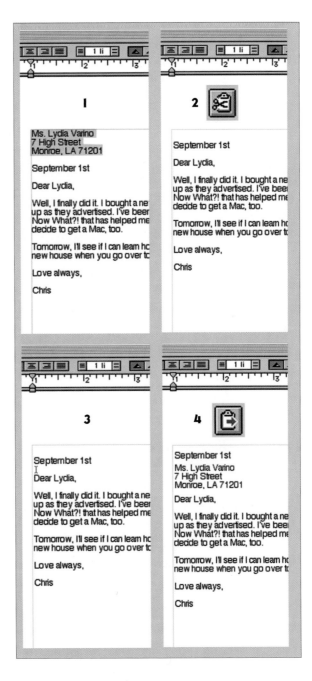

finding files

*Saving means
never having to
say good-bye*

Once you save a file, it will always be on your hard drive.
But the more letters you write, the more cluttered your hard drive
will become. And finding a document that you worked on long ago
can take some time.

Luckily, the Apple menu has an option called Recent Documents
that keeps the names of the 10 most recent files that you've opened.
Select a name, and it will start the application and open the file. As
long as you're only using AppleWorks' word processor, this menu
will contain the 10 most recent letters you've been working on. But
the Apple menu keeps track of all the documents you work with,
which makes it less useful as you learn to use more applications.
For instance, if you're scanning pictures, you may have 5 of those
files on the Recent Documents list and only 5 AppleWorks files.

There are three other ways to find the file you want to open. The
most common on all word processors is to click on the File menu
and choose the Open option. You'll see a window similar to the
Save window. AppleWorks brings you back to the last place you
saved a document. Here you can scroll down or see the items below
the last file on the list by clicking the down arrow next to the list.

Keep things simple
and create a My Files
folder to store your
personal letters. As
you get more experi-
enced, you can create
new folders.

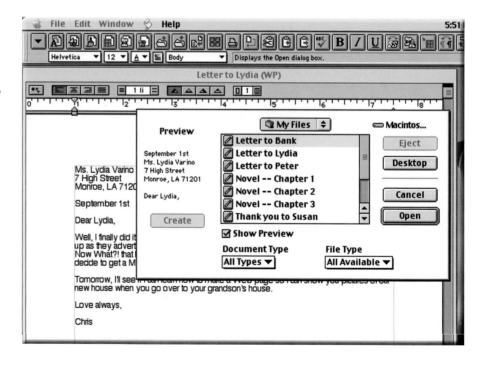

Save As You Go

I was finally getting around to writing up what I had been doing for the last fifteen years for my college's class notes. Doing it on the computer was wonderful because you can edit your writing so easily. No more retyping things over and over again. I was just about done when it started to thunder. The rain was coming down in torrents. I saw the lights flicker and went to check on the house. All was well, but when I got back to my computer the screen was blank—as if I hadn't spent all morning typing up my life. What happened? A call to my son confirmed the worst. My college letter was lost because I hadn't stopped periodically while typing to save it. He said when the lights flickered, my computer probably experienced a power surge and temporarily shut down. When that happens any work that isn't saved is lost. He suggested hitting the save button every five to ten minutes or so.

Pat L., New Smyrna Beach, Florida

HAT IF

You want to open a second file while you're already working on one?

Go ahead and open the second file. The first file you were working on is now behind the second document. You can get back to it by clicking on its grayed-out title bar or by clicking on the Window menu and selecting the first file's name at the bottom of the list.

You want to close the second file?

Click on the Close box at the upper left of the file's window. The first file is back in view.

You can't remember what you named a file?

No problem. Your iMac has a nifty little program called Sherlock that can help you find all sorts of things in your computer, such as files and software programs. To use it, you need to find it. (Yes, it's a bit of a catch-22.) If you have Sherlock as an alias on your desktop, just double-click on it. Otherwise, go up to your Apple menu and scroll down until you hit Sherlock. A Sherlock window will open. Type in what you think you named the file or an unusual word that you remember using in the actual document. Sherlock will display a list of files with that file name or a list of files that contain that weird word. Click on the file that you think is the one you want and Sherlock will tell you where it's hiding. Now close up Sherlock and go to the file, now that you know its name and where it's stored.

45

creating a letter

Writing letters for any occasion

Your word processing software will automatically set the margins, choose the type, and flush left all the text of every letter or document you write. But that doesn't mean you can't change these settings to suit your tastes. Here's how:

CHANGING FONTS AND SIZES:

A Changing fonts: First, highlight the type that you want to change. To select the entire file, hold down the Apple key while pressing the letter A. Click and hold down the mouse button on the small bar under the icons below the File menu (the one that says Helvetica in the picture at right). Drag the cursor down the list to your choice of font and let go of the mouse button. The selection will change to that font. Repeat until you're satisfied with your choice of font.

B Changing font sizes: Same procedure as you used above for changing the font, just click on the box with the number to the right of the font names. Remember that 12 and 10 point are the most common sizes for letters and documents.

C SPACING: To increase the spacing between the lines of your text, highlight the text you want to spread out and click the button to the right of the box that reads "1 li" in the picture at right. To decrease spacing, hit the button to the left of it.

D MARGINS: To change the left margin, drag the rectangular box (with the roof) to the left or right. To change the right margin, drag the pentagon-shaped box (located at the 7-1/2" mark on the ruler) to the left or right.

E ALIGNMENT: You have 4 choices: flush left, centered, flush right, and justified (where text is spaced evenly across the page). If you want to change alignment, simply highlight the text and click on one of these four. All text you write will follow the new alignment.

F INDENTING: To indicate how far you want to indent the first line of each paragraph, drag the down-pointing pentagon to the left or right.

G CREATING EMPHASIS: Don't let your text just lie there if it doesn't reflect the way you feel. You can make text bold, italic, or underlined. Just click on the B, I, or U with your mouse. Go back to your letter. The next words you type will follow your choice.

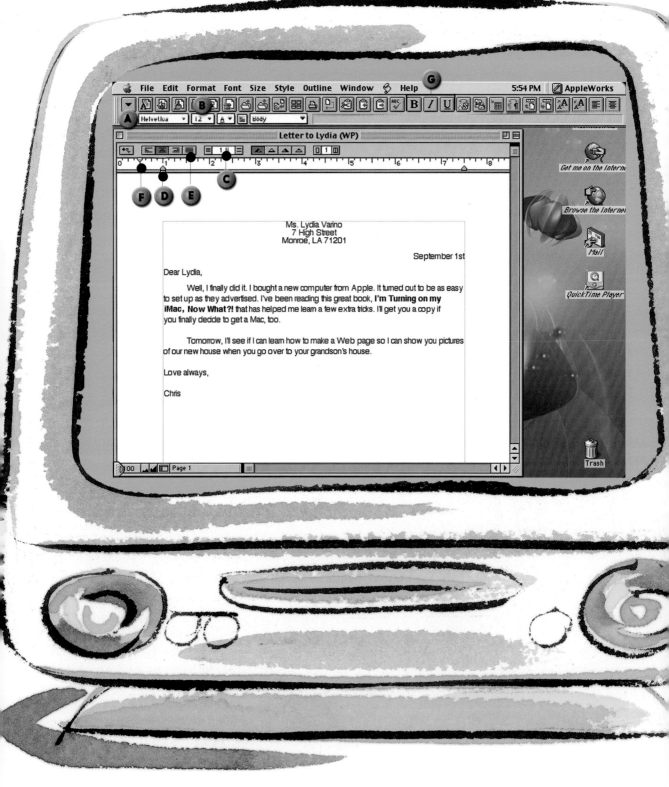

File Edit Format Font Size Style Outline Window   Help   5:54 PM   AppleWorks

Helvetica   12   A   Body

Letter to Lydia (WP)

0   1   2   3   4   5   6   7   8

Ms. Lydia Varino
7 High Street
Monroe, LA 71201

September 1st

Dear Lydia,

Well, I finally did it. I bought a new computer from Apple. It turned out to be as easy to set up as they advertised. I've been reading this great book, **I'm Turning on my iMac, Now What?!** that has helped me learn a few extra tricks. I'll get you a copy if you finally decide to get a Mac, too.

Tomorrow, I'll see if I can learn how to make a Web page so I can show you pictures of our new house when you go over to your grandson's house.

Love always,

Chris

Get me on the Internet

Browse the Internet

Mail

QuickTime Player

Trash

00   Page 1

spelling and more

*Fixing typos
with ease*

One typo on a letter to your bank or on a résumé can sink your chances of getting the loan or landing the job. You're almost certain to make mistakes while typing, but that doesn't mean you have to send it out. You can make sure no misspellings mar your work with some help from your word processor. Almost every word processor includes a spell checker, a feature that checks the spelling of your document or a selection of text.

In AppleWorks, click on the Edit menu and select the Writing Tools option. You'll see another menu that includes the option Check Document Spelling. (Note that this is also where you'll find AppleWorks' thesaurus, so you can vary your vocabulary and not look repetitive.) Click on Check Document Spelling, and AppleWorks presents a window that displays words it doesn't know and suggestions that might be what you meant. Spell checkers are really pretty stupid. They compare all the words in your document with all the words in their dictionaries. When they can't find a match, they question your choice. That means they often don't know the names of people or cities. Fortunately, you can teach the dictionary to recognize words such as your last name by clicking on the Learn button each time it questions a word that you use often.

AppleWorks provides a spell checker and thesaurus. Think of it as having your own in-house editor.

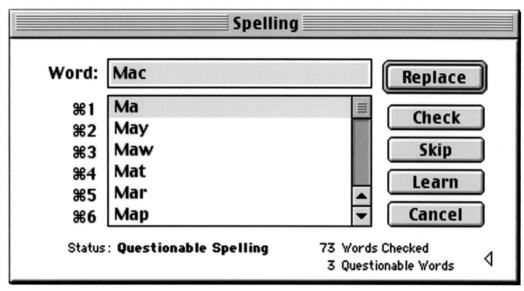

	Spelling	
Word: Mac		**Replace**

⌘1 Ma
⌘2 May
⌘3 Maw
⌘4 Mat
⌘5 Mar
⌘6 Map

Check
Skip
Learn
Cancel

Status: **Questionable Spelling**   73 Words Checked
3 Questionable Words

The spell-checker feature and thesaurus built into most word processors help you craft a more readable letter.

 ## ASK THE EXPERTS

How can I tell how many words I've written?

When you look at the Writing Tools option on AppleWorks' Edit menu, you'll see Word Count on the menu. Selecting it tells you how many words you've written. Other word processors have the same feature.

Whoops! I just told my spell checker to learn a word that I know is misspelled. Can I get it out of the dictionary?

You can edit your dictionary to eliminate any words that shouldn't be there. Click on the Edit menu, select the Writing Tools option, and then select Edit User Dictionary. AppleWorks shows you all the words in your dictionary. Scroll down until you find the offending word, highlight it, and click the Remove button followed by OK. The word is no longer in your dictionary.

printing your letter

Getting that letter onto paper

When you've checked your spelling and read through your document for the final time, get ready to print it. The joy of working with the Macintosh is that "what you see is what you get," that is, the printed page will look like what's staring back at you from the screen. (Among the geek set, this is known as **WYSIWYG**. They actually pronounce this unwieldy string of letters "whizzy-wig.")

So let's get your hands on that masterpiece you've been typing. Click on the File menu and select the Print option. You'll see a window that will look different depending on your printer. Click on the Print button. Your computer will make some noises, and then your printer will start making some more noises (it's kind of like call-and-response singing). You'll see the printer begin to take paper in from one end and kick it out the other with your letter printed on it.

Need multiple copies of your masterpiece? Before clicking on the Print button, look for a box labeled Copies in the printer window. It should be set to 1, but you can type in whatever amount you like, and your iMac will generate exactly that number of duplicates.

Good old Bede spent hours copying his history of the English Church by hand. Today a laser printer could create several copies in minutes.

50

HAT IF

You want to make a change to one page in a report after you've printed out the whole report?

You don't have to print out everything again. Go to the page in question and make the change. When you get to the Print window, look at the option called Pages. Instead of selecting All, click on the button next to the empty box and fill the box with that page's number, which you'll see listed at the bottom of the document window. (For some printers there may be two boxes, so you can define a range of pages to print, for example from 17-18.)

You get an error message when trying to print?

You may not have your printer selected. Click on the Apple menu and select Chooser. Follow the directions from the section "Setting Up Your Printer" in Chapter 1.

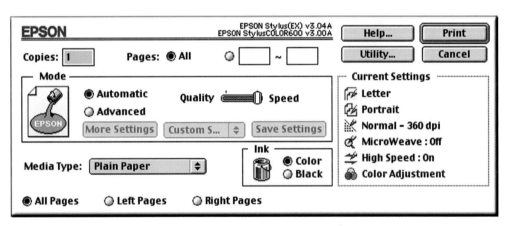

The Print window lets you print one or several copies of your document, individual pages, or the entire work.

now what do I do?

Answers to common problems

How do I start and stop my word processing program?

You've got three options for starting it. If you've used the word processor recently, you'll find that it's listed under the Apple menu's Recent Applications option. If you followed the directions in the Quick Launch box from the Blank Page section earlier in this chapter, you can double-click on the AppleWorks alias on your desktop. If this is your first time using the software, double-click on the Macintosh HD icon on your desktop to open the hard drive. Double-click on the Applications folder and then on the AppleWorks (or other word processor) folder. You'll see the application's icon, which you double-click to start. In all instances you close the program by either clicking on the File menu and selecting the Quit option or by holding down the Apple key on your keyboard while pressing the Q key.

Do I have to start and stop the program each time I want to create a new document?

No, you just have to select the New option from AppleWorks' File menu. This opens a new document. Just remember to save it.

I want to replace a name that I used 10 times in a letter. Is there an easy way to do this?

Most word processors have a Find and Change (or Search and Replace) feature. If you wrote a cover letter for a résumé to one company and want to reuse it for a résumé to a second firm, you'll save yourself time by using Find and Change rather than hunting for every occurrence. This feature also won't miss any references. You, on the other hand, might. In AppleWorks, click on Edit and select the Find/Change option and select Find/Change from the second menu.

Type the first company's name in the box under Find and the second company's name in the one under Change. Click on Find Next, and AppleWorks hunts through the letter for the first time you used the name. Click on the Find and Change option and AppleWorks will change the name to that of the second company and hunt for the next reference. Keep clicking on Find and Change until AppleWorks can't find another reference. Or you can choose to Change All and be done in a jiffy.

How can you use the different keys on the keyboard to move the cursor through a document?

To move the cursor:	Use this key combination:
Right one character	[right arrow]
Left one character	[left arrow]
Up one line	[up arrow]
Down one line	[down arrow]
Previous word	<alt/option>+[left arrow]
Next word	<alt/option>+[right arrow]

Are there different kinds of fonts?

A **font** is a complete collection of letters, punctuation marks, numbers, and special characters with a consistent and identifiable typeface distinguished by weight (such as bold), posture (such as italic), and size (such as HUGE!). There are three basic kinds of fonts: serif, sans serif, and decorative. Serif type has little edges that stick out from the ends of each letter. The classic serif font is Times Roman. Sans serif type has no serifs ("sans" means without in French), such as AppleWorks' default Helvetica—the classic sans serif.

ELPFUL RESOURCES

CONTACTS	BOOKS
Apple Computer Inc. www.apple.com/appleworks 1-800-293-6617	**AppleWorks 5 for Windows and Macintosh: Visual QuickStart Guide** By C. Ann Brown
Microsoft www.microsoft.com/mac 1-425-882-8080	**AppleWorks 5.0 for Dummies** By Bob Levitus
Corel www.corel.com 1-800-772-6735	

Internet

3

In just a few pages the wonders of the Internet are yours for the taking. First there are a few decisions to be made, such as selecting an on-line service provider and choosing a Web browser. What are we talking about? Fret not. All will be explained. And then get ready for serious fun with surfing, shopping, and chatting on-line.

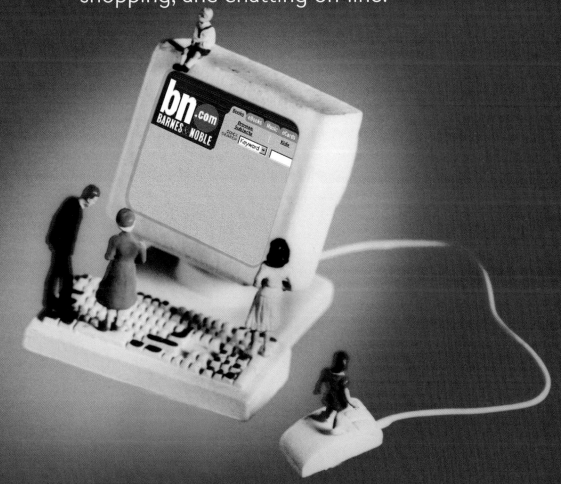

what is the Internet?

*What is it,
and why should
I care?*

So what exactly is the Internet? Well, it's best explained by its nickname, the information superhighway. It's like a huge highway that wraps around the entire world, with zillions of connecting byways, main streets, even dirt tracks. Instead of cars and trucks, little packets of computer information are going along the paths carrying pictures, programs, text, and sounds from anywhere in the world to your computer. Like a real road system, the Internet gets occasional traffic jams, but usually you can go another way.

How do you get onto this highway? You need an **Internet Service Provider** (sometimes called an ISP or On-line Provider; more about those on page 60), which provides an on-ramp for your computer to get onto the highway. Once you're on-line, you can use an electronic mail program to exchange messages, and use a program called a **Web browser** to visit **Web pages.** These pages contain text and pictures. And Web pages also contain **links** to other Web pages. These links are often underlined in blue text; click on a link (more on these later) and you'll find yourself on another Web page. It's these links that gave rise to the Web's name—if you imagine all the links in all the pages as lines, you'd have a mass of threads as intricate as a spiderweb.

If the Internet is the new information superhighway, then you, or rather your computer, are just one of the many cars rattling down it. It doesn't matter whether you are driving a Rolls or a Hyundai. All cars are welcome and all drivers are treated equally.

56

ASK THE EXPERTS

How did the Internet come about?

Back in the 1960s two trends that seem unrelated gave birth to the information superhighway we know today. A few U.S. universities had just developed **supercomputers** (computers that can process huge amounts of data quickly), and the academic world wanted to share in their research and computing power. So the supercomputer centers **networked,** or linked up, with each other and allowed other less powerful computers to access them. Meanwhile, the U.S. Department of Defense wanted to create a channel of communication that could withstand heavy bombing and still be able to carry military intelligence back and forth. So they developed a network too. When the two networks joined together, they became the Internet. Since then millions and millions of smaller networks have joined in, and things have never been the same.

Is the Internet the same thing as the Web?

No, it's not. The Internet is like a network of roads that carry information. The biggest use of the Internet continues to be delivering pieces of electronic mail (E-mail). The World Wide Web also uses the Internet roadway, but instead of simple mail messages, it lets you stop and explore (i.e., browse) the sights in graphic detail, for example, photos of things for sale at on-line stores, news videos, and audio clips.

Who invented the Internet?

It's hard to give the credit to one person or organization, because so many people were involved. The U.S. Department of Defense takes some credit. Vinton Cerf came up with the rules of the road (the Internet **protocols**) that let different computers exchange information. And a physicist named Tim Berners-Lee came up with the idea (and name) of the World Wide Web.

getting connected

To dial up Mom, use the phone; to dial up the world, use a modem

Imagine being able to send letters, photos, videos over the phone. What a world that would be. Well, ahem, it's here. But instead of using your phone, you use your personal computer. Or rather its **modem,** which acts as your computer's phone and dials up the Internet.

Your iMac came with an internal modem built right inside its case, which means you are wired and ready to connect to the Internet. All you have to do is use the good old phone cable that comes with your computer and plug one end of it into the modem **port,** or hole, on the side of your iMac and plug the other end into your home phone jack.

The speed of your modem is calculated as the number of bits per second, or **bps,** it can send. These bits are made up of the data that your modem translates into tones. The tones are then sent over the phone line (just like when you talk on the phone) to another modem that translates the tones back into bits of data.

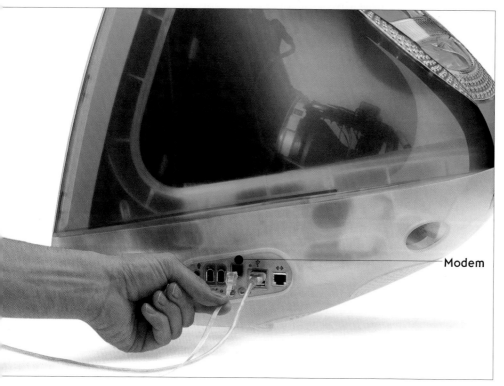

Modem

To connect your internal modem, plug one end of the phone line that came with your iMac into the modem port and the other end into a phone jack. Now you're ready to go. About modem speeds, it's simple: 9,600 bps is very slow; 28,000 bps is slow; 33,600 bps is good; 56,600 bps is best (at least until faster speeds become more common).

ASK THE EXPERTS

What's a fax/modem and how is it different from a modem?

Almost all modems—including your iMac's—are fax/modems, (a nice thing if the person you are trying to send something to isn't on-line.) Having a fax/modem means that you can send and receive faxes from your iMac. Apple includes an application called FaxSTF that lets you receive a fax and then print it out and vice versa.

What's that big phone plug on the side of my iMac?

Although it looks similar to a telephone jack, the larger jack is an **Ethernet connection**. This port allows you to connect to a network—a means for multiple computers to share files—say, if you're in an office. At home you can tap it for an enhanced on-line connection if you sign up for high-speed Internet access with your cable company or a digital subscriber line (DSL) provider. Both cable and DSL will provide you with a special modem that connects to the Ethernet port and gives you speed more than 25 times as fast as your modem—for a price. Currently, so called broadband providers charge a minimum of $40 per month.

Can I use the phone while I'm on-line?

No. If you pick up another extension while you're on-line, you'll hear lots of screeching sounds. Your iMac may also lose its connection. The click from call waiting can also throw you off-line. Most Internet service software allows you to automatically dial the *70 combination that disables call waiting in the U.S. If you've got a teenager who's eager to use the phone, consider installing another line for your iMac. Most local phone companies charge a small monthly fee for the extra line.

going on-line

Learn about the new phone companies of the Internet

To use your telephone, you need the phone company to provide you with phone service. The same goes for your modem. But instead of Ma Bell connecting you, you need to sign up with a company that will provide Internet service—either an **Internet Service Provider** (or ISP) or an **on-line service.** America Online, Earthlink, CompuServe, and the Microsoft Network are some of the main ones.

What is Internet service? Well, it basically gives you access via your phone line to a big Internet computer that is linked to other Internet computers all over the world. Either type of service will give you the telephone number of a computer near you that your modem can dial into to provide access to the Internet. (You want to dial a local number so you won't have to pay long-distance charges each time you go on-line.) Some providers charge a flat monthly fee, while others charge by the hour. (Part of this service includes an E-mail account. More on that later.)

Regardless of the type of service you choose, you will need to come up with two important things: your user name and password. A user name can be your last name or a made-up name. To protect your Internet privacy, we suggest you use a made-up user name, perhaps a nickname or your initials. Just make sure you won't mind giving it out as your E-mail address. Your password can be any word or set of numbers you can remember easily.

Think of your on-line service provider as your own personal operator who puts your calls through over the Internet.

SK THE EXPERTS

Can someone eavesdrop on me while I'm on-line?

The risk of someone tracing where you surf on-line or reading what you write in chat rooms is pretty remote. For it to happen, a secret program has to be hidden in a suspect Web site—the kind run by shady characters. This is one of the many reasons why you should not visit Web sites listed in E-mail messages from people you don't know. Just clicking on it could give them the access they need to your E-mail account.

If I get an internet account, can someone get into my computer files without my knowing it?

Any unauthorized entry into someone else's computer files is called **hacking** and is a federal offense. Hackers usually are not interested in private computers; they are after security holes in big Web sites. You can reduce the tiny risk of getting "hacked" by not staying on-line for long stretches at a time, say overnight.

Can I get a computer virus from the Internet?

Yes, computer viruses do abound on-line. A **virus** is a nuisance program that can infect software programs or files on your hard drive. They can cause your computer to crash (stop working unexpectedly) or they can come with a "payload" that could do anything from making it impossible to save files to erasing all the files on your hard drive! To protect your computer from viruses, you should purchase antivirus software; it's available at most computer stores. Once you install it (see page 25), the antivirus software will start up when you start your iMac and run constantly, ready to intercept any virus that comes on the scene. To be safe, don't open E-mail attachments from people you don't know or trust, especially if the attachment is a software program. (You can also download or copy free antivirus software from the Web.) Visit these Web sites for help: **www.download.com** or **www.tucows.com.**

using an ISP

*Going local
has its
advantages*

You've probably seen advertisements in your local paper exclaiming how you can connect to the Internet; just call this number and find out how. The phone number listed is an Internet Service Provider, or ISP. These are businesses that supply Internet access to people like you and me as well as businesses. Most ISPs are local mom-and-pop operations, but some are large national or international corporations. They will send you their software, which you will load (see page 25) in order to use their service.

To find a local ISP, check your phone book under Internet Services. (If you don't see any listed in your region, then you'll need to use a national On-line Service Provider; see the following page). Check out the various benefits and prices of the ISPs in your area. For example, some bill you by the month, others by the year.

Most local ISPs offer local news on their welcome page. This ISP, Computer.Net out of Westchester, NY, also gives the weather.

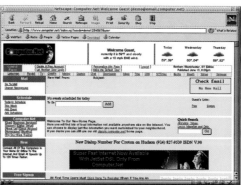

Once you've chosen your ISP, they will give you the following information so you can get started:

- First, their Internet phone number, which your computer's modem will dial into (that is called an **access phone number**). Remember to make sure this is a local number.

- Next, they will give you the Internet "address" of their computer, which is called a **domain name server** address or DNS (usually 4 sets of numbers like 070.13.205.204).

- Finally, you will give them your **user name** and **password,** so think about these before you call them.

STEP BY STEP: ISP

With the Internet Setup Assistant, setting up an account with an ISP requires reading some instructions, typing in some information, and watching it all happen.

1. Double-click on the "Get me on the Internet" icon with the italic writing on your iMac's desktop. This shortcut will configure the ISP software that Apple has already installed on your iMac.

2. Click on Yes in the Internet Setup Assistant window when it asks "Would you like to set up your iMac to use the Internet?"

3. It will ask you, "Do you already have an Internet account?" If you've already arranged for service with an ISP in your neighborhood, click on Yes and provide the assistant with the information it requires, including your user name, password, your phone number, the phone number to reach the local ISP, and something called a DNS number.

FIRST PERSON DISASTER

On-line/Off-line

All I wanted to do on my computer was be able to get on-line so I could check out the action on some of these auction sites. I am a collector of wines and more and more wine auctions are being held on-line. So I dialed up a local provider that my neighbor uses and got connected. Got all the information. Typed it all in. The DSN number, the ISP phone number, my number. You name it. When I was finished I restarted my computer, ready to start wheeling and dealing at one of the biggest wine auctions that afternoon. Nothing. Couldn't get on-line. Kept getting a message saying insufficient connection, try again. I kept trying and trying. I called the ISP provider and asked them what to do. We went over everything. All the numbers I had typed in were correct. So I tried again. And again. Still nothing. Needless to say, I missed the auction. Later that night, I called my ISP again to tell them to cancel my account, when they asked if I had added the number one in front of my area code and phone number. Yes, of course. "Oh, that's the problem. You don't need the number 1." Oh. Swell.

Sam R., Madison, Wisconsin

using an on-line service

Going for the big time

So you think you want to go the on-line services route. It's a good way to get started using the Internet without getting too technical. Plus, your iMac comes with on-line service software already installed or at least some type of installation setup, so you're almost there.

If friends and family prod you into joining AOL, there are many reasons you should follow their advice. First of all, Apple includes the AOL software on your iMac. Second, AOL lets you connect, browse the Web, read E-mail, chat, join discussion groups, and much more. You can do all these things with an ISP, but you'll use different applications to do each task, several of which you'll need to retrieve from the Web and install yourself. Does the second option sound kind of scary? Then AOL is your best bet. Oh, yeah. AOL also gives you five screen names—its word for user names. That means you'll have five separate E-mail addresses, enough for most families.

To configure the AOL software that is already installed on your iMac:

1. Double-click on the Macintosh HD.

2. Double-click on the Internet folder. You'll see an AOL icon there in the Internet window (actually, you should notice that it's an alias to the AOL application that is in the America Online folder).

3. Double-click on the icon, and AOL begins asking you a series of questions that steer you through the registration process.

Some on-line providers such as America Online let you access your E-mail right from their home page. See that little Mailbox icon on the upper left? Click on it, and it will immediately take you to your E-mail account.

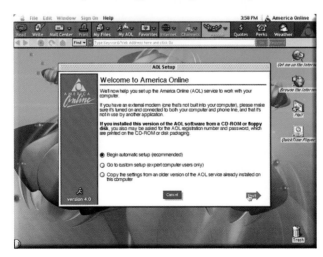

ASK THE EXPERTS

I just got a CD in the mail from an on-line service promoting their software. How does that work?

The CD is basically a mini-trial of how the on-line service works. All you need is a phone line and a modem, and you're in business. They are giving you a free trial with a certain number of minutes "free" on-line to research, send E-mail. If you like it, you can convert to a paying account unless you cancel. (You can't use those free minutes to augment an existing account.) To install the software from a CD, see page 25 for help.

I live in a rural area. Is there on-line service for me?

The chances of finding a local service provider are improving as the Internet continues to grow. You can always go with a big on-line service. Just make sure they have a local phone number available in your area. If the closest number they have is a long-distance one, you will run up your phone bill by paying for long-distance connections or the extra fees they often tack on to utilize a toll-free number.

I don't know which way is better, an ISP or on-line service?

There are pros and cons to each one, many of which will change over time as on-line companies continue to improve their services. But for starters, ISPs are typically local outfits that can provide you with local service. That means anything from a home page that has local weather and movie information to easy access to a tech person to answer your tech questions. For some, local is nice; for others who work at 3 a.m. when the tech person is sleeping, it's a problem. On-line providers offer national service with a slew of tech people to help you. That said, they also can suffer from on-line congestion because so many of their customers are trying to get on-line at peak hours, say, 7–10 p.m. Good advice: Compare prices and services before you sign up.

getting around the Web

If you wanna surf, you gotta use a board

You've got a modem and a service provider. Now what?
You need something called a **browser.** That's the computer name for software that allows you to navigate the Internet. Think of it as the surfboard that allows you to surf the Web. Happily, your iMac comes with three browsers installed, the one included in America Online and stand-alone browsers from Microsoft or Netscape.

To open your browser, simply click on its icon on your desktop. When your browser software opens, it will most likely open to its home page. It usually contains an index, search options, and connections to other Web pages. Take a look at that home page. Do you see text that is underlined? It is called a **hyperlink** (or sometimes just link). If you click on the underlined text, it will automatically "link" you to a different page or perhaps another Web site. If you click on a link, don't like it, and want to go back to where you started, click on the Back button on the Web browser button bar (located at the top of your screen). Notice that after you have clicked on a link, it is a different color—letting you know you have been there before.

HAT IF

You can't find the browser software?

Open the Macintosh hard drive and double-click on the Internet Applications folder, inside which you'll find folders for Microsoft's Internet Explorer, Netscape's Navigator, and America Online.

You want to print out a Web page?

Click the Print button on the Web browser button bar.

Your Web page doesn't display right away and you see a page that says it didn't come up properly?

Click the Refresh button on the Web browser button bar.

You want to install something different from what you have?

Believe it or not, America Online, Microsoft, and Netscape (the three programs Apple loads on your iMac) do not have a monopoly on browsers. If you want to try an alternative such as Opera (**www.opera.com**), you can download it from the Web. Once the file's finished downloading, double-click on it and follow the instructions on-screen.

just browsin'

Many people equate the World Wide Web with the Internet. The Web is really only one part of the Net, but it's the friendly face that makes the Internet easy to use—combining text, graphics, video, and sound with simple navigation tools. The Web consists of millions of Web pages that are connected through links. Here's an overview of two popular Web browsers: AOL and Microsoft Internet Explorer.

A Link Click on this colored (and generally underlined) text and your browser takes you to another page related to this text.

B Address or URL The Web page that you are currently viewing. You can type over it and hit the Return key to go to another address.

C Home Takes you to the home page defined in your browser. By default, Internet Explorer takes you to Apple.com and AOL takes you to AOL.com.

D Favorites A collection of your favorite Web sites that you ask your browser to remember.

E Stop If one site's page is taking too long to load, you can stop it and type in another location.

F Back Click here to go back to the last page you visited.

G Forward Forward returns you to the page you were visiting before you clicked back.

H Refresh Reloads the page you've been viewing—for instance, when you want to update changes in the stock market.

I Text Box Put your cursor here to type in information to send to a Web page, for example, when searching a site.

J Search Button Click on this just as you would any other option on your iMac.

On the next page are two browsers at work: AOL at the top and Microsoft's Internet Explorer at the bottom. Notice that while their buttons are in different places, the Web page they are showing (HotBot) stays the same.

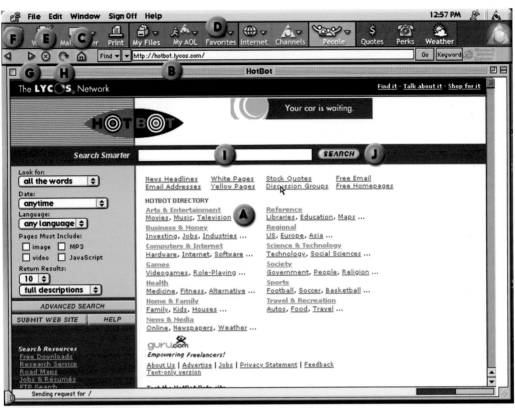

researching on-line

Surfing the web is as easy as catching a wave

The Web continues to grow with more and more pages each day. In order to find what you seek, there are companies out there that have created user-friendly **search engines** (programs that find things by using key words) to help you search **databases** (computer files full of information) that track pages from all over the world. Some names of popular search engines are Yahoo!, Excite, AltaVista, and Looksmart. Here's how search engines work: If you want to look up information on puppies, you would simply type the key word puppies in the Search box and click the Search button. You will then see a list of underlined links (from news articles about puppies to sites that sell puppy food) to choose from (possibly more than one page of them). Click on the particular link that interests you, and away you go.

This is the home page or welcome page of the search engine Yahoo! Type the key words that describe what you are researching in the Search box and click on the Search button. Voilà—instant info.

There's another way to search. You can go right to a specific site if you know its address. What is a **Web address**? It tells your computer where a company, an organization, even schools are on the Web. Instead of using the Search box, you go up to the Address bar and type in the Web address and press Enter. You should immediately be taken to the home page of that address.

Web address

Search button

Search box
(Type in the key word such as puppies in this box, then click the Search button.)

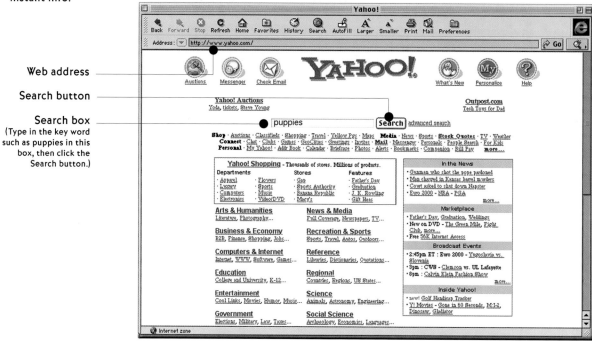

ASK THE EXPERTS

What do "http" and "www" stand for?

Get ready for a little technical lingo. HTTP stands for Hypertext Transfer Protocol. Basically, it's the code that allows you to send and receive stuff over the Web. You don't need to type in the http:// when you are browsing the Web; your browser will automatically do it for you. Not so with everything else in the Web address, including www., which stands for the World Wide Web. Most companies have the www. before their name, and you must type it in the address field.

What are the slashes and dots doing in an Internet address?

The slashes and dots between words are providing specific location information about the address, a bit like a zip code.

How do I mark a Web site to come back to it again later?

In Internet Explorer, choose Favorites, then Add to Favorites; in Netscape Navigator, choose Bookmarks, then Add to Bookmarks; in AOL, click on the heart icon in the upper right of every Web page. Click OK when AOL asks you if you want to add it to your Favorite Places. The favorite or bookmark will get added to the Favorites or Bookmarks list that you see when you click on it. When you click on one of the Web pages on the list, the Web site will immediately open in your browser.

What does URL mean?

It's technospeak for a site's Internet address, such as yahoo.com or www.whitehouse.gov. If you must know, URL stands for Uniform Resource Locator.

WEB ADDRESSES

A Web address is the address you type in to get to a place on the Internet. Most Web addresses start with www for World Wide Web, then dot (typed as a period), then the name of the organization, then dot and an abbreviation. For instance, the Web address for Barnes & Noble is: www.bn.com. For the Public Broadcasting System: www.PBS.org. The last three letters of the address tell you something about the site.

.com   a company
.org   a non-profit
       organization
.net   a network provider
.edu   school or university
.gov   U.S. government
.mil   the military

shopping on-line

No more long lines at the cash register

Ever go shopping and find a parking spot right away, walk directly to the right department, and then discover that the item you are looking for is not there? Well, those days are gone. You can shop on-line, find what you want, and get it mailed to you; and if they don't happen to have the item right now, they'll mail it when they do. And chances are it will be cheaper than in the store. How come? The item is almost always less expensive to make up for the extra charge of mailing it to you. All you need is access to the Internet, a browser, and a credit card.

Just as in the real world, there are a number of different ways to shop on the Internet: 1) directly from the manufacturer such as **ibm.com**; 2) from retail stores like **walmart.com**; 3) from cyber-space-only stores like **eToys.com**; 4) from Internet malls like **shop-now.com**; 5) from on-line auctions like **ebay.com**; and 6) from catalogs like **landsend.com**. Some things never change: When you first get to a site you can expect to see specials, sales, and a pitch—just as you would at a local store.

Most on-line stores provide you with a shopping cart—an on-line equivalent of its namesake. You click through the store looking at products. Select those that interest you, and the Web site's software adds it to your shopping cart. When you've found everything you need, you click on the checkout link and the site asks you for your name, a shipping address, and your credit card information. Select how you want it sent (via standard post or overnight delivery) and your purchases will begin winging their way to you.

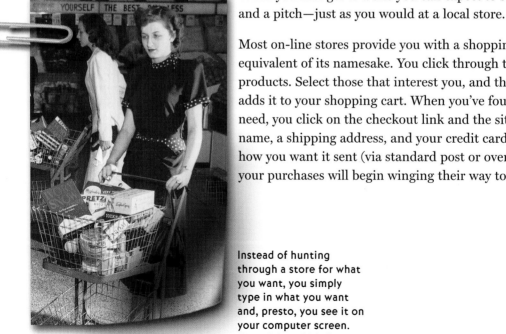

Instead of hunting through a store for what you want, you simply type in what you want and, presto, you see it on your computer screen. One click and it's in your virtual shopping cart.

SK THE EXPERTS

How can I search for a particular item on a shopping site?

You can usually search for products by category, but it can be faster to use the site's search box. Type in the word(s) that describe the product, manufacturer, or type of goods, and click the Go or Search button. Review the list of items and click on the appropriate link.

How safe is my credit card number on-line?

When secure sites ask for your credit card number, they encrypt it, or scramble it, in code so that no one can read it who isn't allowed. Your browser uses symbols to let you know if a site is secure or not. Internet Explorer uses a padlock—if it's open, then the site is not secure. Netscape uses a key—if the key is broken, then the site is not secure.

Are my shopping habits ever tracked ?

Often when you buy things on-line, the sellers put a "**cookie**" into your virtual shopping cart. The cookie links your name to your purchase so the seller knows what types of goods and services you are interested in.

73

auctions on-line

Going...going... gone!

Imagine you've got a closetful of stuff you don't use anymore. (Not too hard, is it?) Sure, you could hold a garage sale, but if you're tired of tire kickers trying to haggle you down, you can find a good home for more or less anything by holding an on-line auction. And once you've freed up space in that closet, you can bid on other people's unappreciated treasures to fill it up again!

Sure, dealing with strangers can be a leap of faith, but auction sites have a good self-policing system in place. Sellers and buyers build a reputation—people they do business with can leave electronic feedback about how friendly or fast a buyer or seller is. The more positive feedback you see, the more confident you can feel about doing business with someone. And if a deal goes bad, the auction site intervenes: Descriptions and bids are legally binding contracts. If there's any funny business, the auction site will usually revoke membership. Bad customers don't stick around long, so you can bid and sell with a fair amount of confidence.

There are a number of auction sites to choose from, and the list just keeps growing. For starters, check out **www.ebay.com** (shown here) or **auctions.yahoo.com.**

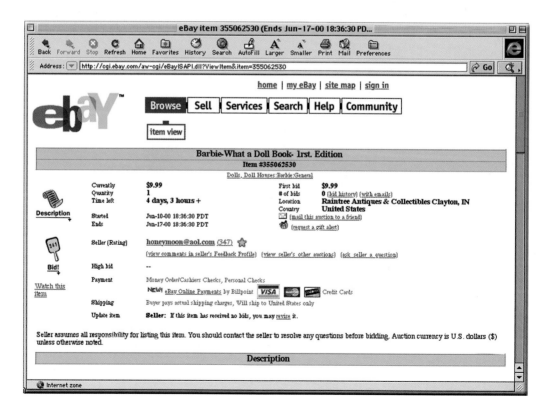

STEP BY STEP: AUCTIONING

1. Sign up with an on-line auction site. Click on the site's "Join" link and be prepared to enter your real name, address, and E-mail address, as well as a screen name and password. If you're selling, you'll probably need to enter a credit card number or arrange to send a check to the company so that they can deduct an "insertion fee" (usually between a quarter and a dollar) for listing your item. They'll also want a percentage of the final bidding price—no more than 5 percent.

2. Once you've joined, you can put up items for sale. Sellers should set a realistic starting price (aim low to encourage bidders, but not so low that you'd be upset if you got only the opening bid). Compose an accurate description of the item (and be up-front about any faults or flaws—buyers don't like surprises). It's also helpful to find out how much it will cost to ship the item before the auction.

3. Buyers can search for items by entering key words (lace curtains, Beanie Baby, Tiffany lamps, and so on) in the site's Search box. The matching list is sorted by date, with the auctions about to close at the top. If an item seems interesting, click on it.

4. When the auction closes, the auction site will send an E-mail to the highest bidder and seller. These two must figure out the details by themselves in a fixed time frame—usually a week. They work out how to pay (check, money order, or whatever), how to deliver, and how to do what they've agreed on. Many sellers insist on waiting until an out-of-state check clears before delivering—so the buyer may wait a few weeks after the last bid before seeing the goods.

5. When the goods arrive, it's helpful to leave a feedback message about the experience at the site. A good seller deserves praise, and other buyers deserve to know if a seller is slow or not very communicative.

BARGAIN HUNTING

Sites like **www.priceline.com** and **www.hagglezone.com** are places where businesses provide goods that they're prepared to sell below retail price. You, as a buyer, can search for something you want and name a price you're prepared to pay. The company can take or leave your offer, so if you don't bid too low (or if the company has overstocked and is desperate to empty its warehouses), you can usually get a great deal.

chatting on-line

Having a silent conversation with people who have similar interests

Get passionate about a hobby or a sports team, and you want to share your enthusiasm with someone. Trouble is, fellow enthusiasts are often few and far between. That's where on-line chat rooms can help. Chatting on the Net isn't exactly talking. It's more like writing notes back and forth to a friend in grade school, except this time you don't have to do it behind the teacher's back.

On-line services have built-in chat rooms where you can talk about virtually anything with other people who share your service. If you have an ISP and are looking for a chat room using your Web browser, you can find a Chat link on most of the World Wide Web search engine sites (refer to page 70). You can also access these sites from your on-line service, but you need to use the Web link instead of your service's chat option.

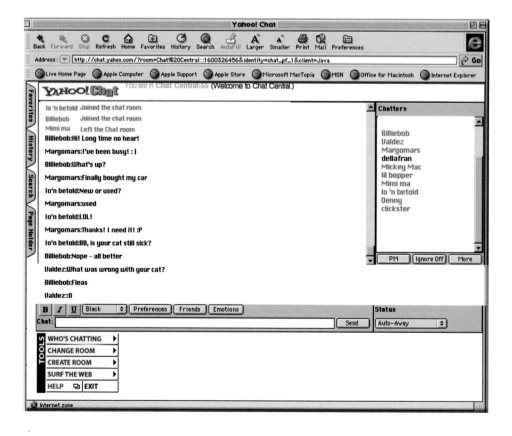

STEP BY STEP: CHATTING

To see how chatting works, try Yahoo!'s free service. Its features are similar to those of other chat sites.

1. Type **chat.yahoo.com** in the Address bar of your Web browser.

2. If you haven't already registered with Yahoo!, click on Sign Up for Yahoo!'s Chat option. (This also signs you up for a free Yahoo! E-mail account and access to all the other features of the portal.) Write down your new Yahoo! I.D. and the password that you chose.

3. When you're done with registration, type in your I.D. and password to sign in.

4. Click on a chat topic that interests you.

5. Yahoo! displays chat messages in the message area. To add to the conversation, type your message in the box below the message area and click the Send button. Your message will be sent to all the other users. Have fun!

6. To end your chat session, type in another address on the Address bar or click on your Home button.

ASK THE EXPERTS

Why does the conversation seem unrelated to the topic?

Patience. Entering a chat room is like coming to a cocktail party that's already under way. Chat participants may be in the middle of conversations that have taken a silly turn. Just follow along for a few minutes and look for an opening to introduce yourself. Like all good conversationalists, the chat participants may ask you about yourself (where you're from and how the weather is there) before they ask your opinion about the topic at hand.

How can I join a chat on AOL if I haven't signed up with AOL?

At **aol.com/community/directory.html** you can click on the AOL Instant Messenger link to download free software that lets you participate in AOL chats without subscribing to its service.

live on-line

If you want to chat with people who use America
Online's service as well as people on the Internet at large, your best
bet is to get America Online's Instant Messenger program, also
known as AIM. Don't worry—it's free, and you don't need to subscribe
to the company's on-line service to use it.

1. Go to aol.com to download the AIM program. Make a note of
   where you download the program—when you've finished downloading it, you'll need to find the program using Finder and
   double-click on it to install the software.

2. When you install the software, it will ask you to pick a screen
   name and password. The screen name you pick will appear on
   all the messages you type. Make a note of it and pass it around
   to your friends as your new AOL/AIM I.D. And get their screen
   names too.

3. Every time you get on-line, AIM will start up and let your buddies know that you're available for a chat.

4. To see whether your buddies are on-line, add them to your
   "Buddy List"—all you need to know is their screen names. In
   AIM's Buddy List window, click on the List Setup tab and
   click on Buddies. Select Add Buddy and type in your
   buddy's screen name. Then click on the On-line tab.

5. If your friend is on-line, you'll see his or her name in the
   Buddy List window. Double-click on it. A new window will
   appear. Type a quick greeting and press the Enter key.

6. When your friend sees you're starting a chat, he or she will
   send a reply. (Don't be impatient—they may be away from their
   computer when you first say "hi.") You can then hold a "conversation" by typing messages and hitting the Enter key to send
   them.

now what do I do?

Answers to common problems

What is downloading?

Downloading is geekspeak for transferring a copy of a file from an on-line computer to your iMac. You download files that you want to store—say, a copy of Shakespeare's sonnets—or programs that you want to install. If the latter, only download the Macintosh version of any applications, such as the free AOL Instant Messenger.

I forgot my password. How do I find it?

If you installed an ISP account with the Internet Setup Assistant, don't worry. It's stored on your iMac, so you don't have to remember it each time you go on-line. It's a good idea to have the password handy, so contact your ISP's customer service department and ask them to give it to you. Write it down and put it in a safe place. With America Online, you'll have to contact its customer service department.

What does it mean when I get a message that says "The page cannot be displayed?"

There are three reasons that a Web page doesn't show up on your screen. It was removed from the Web site by the Webmaster, traffic across the Web is too bogged down to display it, or you've tried to access a private page that's password protected by a company. Of course, you could also have mistyped the address. First, check that you spelled the address correctly. Second, click on your browser's Refresh button. Finally, try the link later in the day to confirm that traffic wasn't the problem. Otherwise try another site.

Why do I sometimes get a busy signal when I try to connect to the Internet?

Your ISP or on-line provider probably has too many people connected at once. Keep trying the number until you get through and then look up more access numbers on your ISP's Web site (or in Member Services on AOL). Next time you get a busy signal, try to get through on another phone number.

Why does the connection to my ISP suddenly stop working?

Your modem may have had a poor connection to your ISP. If your ISP can't "hear" your modem clearly, it will drop the connection. Contact your ISP's customer service department if this happens frequently.

What do I do if I have call waiting on my regular phone line?

Call waiting will cause static on your Internet connection, which will most likely disconnect you. So before you go on-line, dial *70 to block out incoming calls.

Do manufacturers get information about me from what I buy?

Yes. It's called a cookie. A cookie is a small file that some Web sites insert onto your hard drive when you visit them for the first time. The information stored in the cookie enables that site to compile information about your browsing habits and purchases to help them serve you better. They can also pass this information on to other Web sites. Virtual shopping carts need cookies to complete your on-line order.

What are some of the most popular search engines?

AltaVista	altavista.com
Excite	excite.com
GoTo	goto.com
HotBot	hotbot.com
InfoSeek	infoseek.com
Lycos	lycos.com
Northern Light	northernlight.com
Yahoo!	yahoo.com
Looksmart	looksmart.com

HELPFUL RESOURCES

CONTACTS	BOOKS
America Online www.aol.com 1-888-265-8003	**The Internet for Dummies** By John R. Levine, Carol Baroudi, and Margaret Levine Young
Earthlink 1-404-815-0770	
Microsoft www.microsoft.com/mac/ie/default.asp 1-425-882-8080	

E-Mail

4

All you really want to do is E-mail the family, maybe some friends. It's why you bought the book, right? So learn how easy it is to get an E-mail account. How to receive and send messages and attachments. How to create an address book. It's easy. The days of letters and stamps are over.

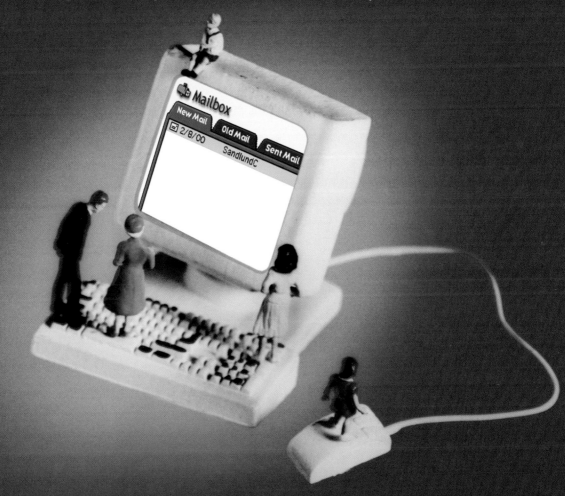

getting an
E-mail account

*Your own
mailbox in
cyberspace*

Chances are that you got your iMac just to get on-line—
meaning you want access to the Internet. And the number one reason you want to get on-line is to send and receive **E-mail** from
friends and family. E-mail is computerese for electronic mail, a
message that you can address like a letter to someone else to read.
E-mail is how you can send birthday greetings to a friend, pass
along pictures of a newborn, forward a chapter of that new book
you're writing, and even send a video from your vacation.

By signing up with an **Internet Service Provider** (**ISP**) or **on-line
service** (see page 62), you automatically receive an E-mail account.
But to read and write E-mail, you're going to need special software—with two exceptions discussed below. Most of this software
is already available in the Internet folder of your iMac's hard drive.
If not, your ISP will gladly send it to you. Should you sign up with
a company like America Online (also known as AOL), the ability to
write E-mail is part of AOL's basic software.

Internet Service
Providers or on-
line services auto-
matically give you
an E-mail account
upon registration.

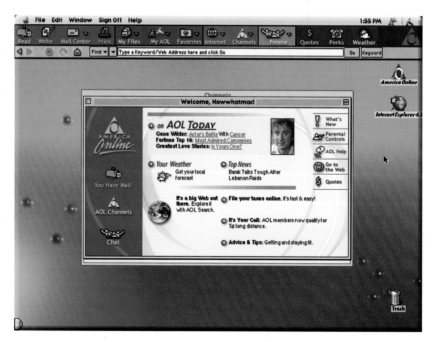

ASK THE EXPERTS

How safe is E-mail?

E-mail is like a postcard. Someone who wants to pry into your private life can read your E-mail notes. Also, E-mail is very easy to forward. A joke that you thought your friend would find funny might not be so funny to the person he or she sends it to. And that person can trace the message back to you. Your best bet is to play it safe with what you say in your messages.

What is spam?

Another worry is whether you'll start receiving unsolicited E-mails from marketers or porn exploiters, called spam. There's no guarantee that your E-mail address will remain out of these people's hands, but contact your ISP to help you shield your mailbox from spam.

How can companies afford to offer free E-mail?

Sites like HotMail and Yahoo! provide E-mail as a service by selling ads on their Web sites for you to view. They also attach a small advertisement about themselves on every message that you send. Companies like Freei.net provide free E-mail, but you have to give them information about yourself so they can flash ads at you.

your E-mail address

Why stand in line at the post office?

The basics of sending an E-mail aren't that different from sending a letter through the post office. You address the envelope, write a message, and then you send it off from the post office. With E-mail you do all of this on your computer screen. Progress, eh?

To send or receive E-mail, you first need an E-mail address. E-mail is made up of two parts. You've probably seen E-mail addresses like billg@microsoft.com. (Yes, that's Microsoft founder Bill Gates's real E-mail address. He actually has a computer program screen all his messages for him.) The first part of the address, billg, is the name—in this case it stands for Bill Gates. The second part of the address is separated from the first by the @, or at, sign. It's a pretty elegant way of linking a name to a location, in this case, Bill Gates at Microsoft. The second half of the address is called the **domain name** and it represents where you are—virtually speaking, that is. So someone with an America Online address would be @aol.com and someone with a free HotMail account would be @hotmail.com. The .com simply stands for company.

Your message needs to be addressed correctly to get where it needs to go. Unfortunately, in cyberspace, there's no postman to figure out that a building's apartment 60 is really apartment 6E. If you make a mistake, you will probably get a message back from your ISP saying your E-mail was "not delivered." Check the address and try again.

SK THE EXPERTS

Why do some people use lowercase letters in their E-mail addresses?

E-mail addresses are not case sensitive. The computer will read a capital letter or a lowercase letter the same way, so don't worry about whether you should capitalize a name or not.

Can I just have letters and numbers in my E-mail address or can I use other characters?

The only other allowable characters in an E-mail address are periods, underscores, and hyphens. For example, mary.prankster; mary_prankster; or mary-prankster. You can't use ampersands (&) or slashes (/) or asterisks (*).

What is snail mail?

Because it takes so long to send a letter through the good old U.S. mail compared to sending electronic mail via the Internet, computer techie-types came up with the expression "snail mail" when talking about letters that go through the mail.

getting E-mail messages

You've got mail!

So now that you've got an E-mail account, who's going to send you messages? Well, before you even tell anyone of your new on-line address, your Internet Service Provider will send you a welcome message. Different E-mail programs alert you to new E-mail with audio and visual clues. With America Online, for instance, you'll hear the expression that's now synonymous with its system ("You've got mail!") and see the Read icon underneath the Apple menu change to a mailbox with letters coming out of it. Microsoft and Netscape's programs play a *ding* whenever a new message arrives. When you look in these applications' **inboxes,** the new messages are in bold. An inbox is a window that acts like the place in big offices where the mail department drops memos and mail.

To read your E-mail, double-click on the most recent message, and you'll be able to read it. When you're done with it, you can delete it or click on the next arrow to read the next message. With AOL, mail you've read is put into the Old Mail folder of your mailbox. With Microsoft Outlook and Netscape Communicator it stays in your inbox until you delete it, when it is moved to the program's Deleted Items folder.

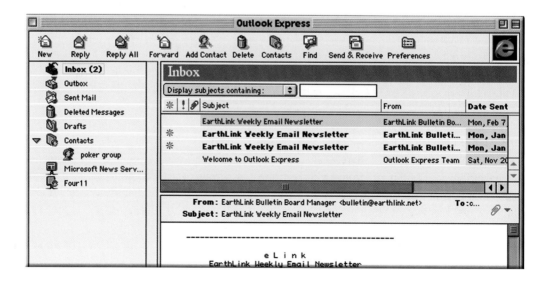

ASK THE EXPERTS

How do I reply directly to a message?

Once you open and read a message, you can reply to the person who sent you the message (known as the **sender**) by clicking on Reply or Reply to All, if there was more than one sender.

How do I open an E-mail attachment?

If an E-mail message has an attached file, you'll see a small icon next to the message in your inbox. In Outlook Express, the icon is a paper clip; in AOL it's a box with a blue floppy disk behind it. After you open your E-mail message, you will see another icon of the attached file somewhere in your message. In Outlook Express you can double-click on the icon of the attached file and it will open. In AOL, click on the attachments tab, and you'll see an icon of the attached file; you will then need to drag it to your desktop where you can open it later. If the attached file is a text file, Appleworks should be able to open it. If it's got **.sit** next to the file name, it's been compressed. See page 94 for more information.

See page 94 for more information.

SENDING ATTACHMENTS

You can send any file that is stored in your computer—your gardening newsletter, a scanned photo of the kids (see page 108). To do it, first create an E-mail message, then find the file and attach it. In Outlook Express, for example, click on the Add Attachments icon. A dialogue box will appear to help you find your file. Once found, click Add, then click Done. You'll see an icon of the file in your E-mail message. Click Send and off it all goes.

(see page 108)

FIRST PERSON DISASTER
E-Mailer beware

I love my computer. It's made time-consuming tasks like writing letters to friends and family easy. I used to write these long letters, now I just E-mail away and bing off it goes. It's amazing. (I wonder if this is how my grandmother felt when she took her first ride in a Model T Ford.) The only bad thing is that I get a lot of unsolicited E-mail—mostly from people wanting to sell me stuff. But there was one E-mail I'll never forget. It said it was from a discount travel agency. If I opened up the link (the underlined part) in the E-mail message, it would link me to a super discount site for Hawaii. Of course, I did just that. Instead of Hawaii, it kept repeating the message over and over again and I couldn't stop it. Even when I turned off my computer and restarted it, the message was still there. I was so unnerved I called my service provider who told me that the link to the discount site had a virus which had attacked my computer. They suggested I buy anti-virus software and install it and it would kill the virus. I did and was back up and running. The moral: don't open any links from any E-mailer you don't know. It's just like my grandmother used to tell us kids, don't get in a car with a stranger.

Molly G., Darien, Connecticut

89

writing E-mail

*Stationery
not required*

Writing E-mail is a lot like writing a memo in an office.
At least that's what the people who invented it intended. That's
why E-mail has memo-like elements. Here are some of the basics
of writing an E-mail message:

A TO: This is where you put the E-mail address of the person to
whom you are sending a message.

B CC or Copy: Here's where you put the address of anyone you
want to receive a copy of the message (from the days of memos
that had carbon copies).

C Subject: A place to explain what you're writing about. E-mail
programs generally display the sender's E-mail address, the subject, and the date. An informative subject line tells the recipient
that your message is not spam and gives some idea of how
important the message is.

D Style: Adjust the look of the body of your E-mail message as if
it were a letter. (See Chapter 2's section "Creating a Letter"—
the features are almost identical.) Note that some systems only
accept plain text, so your formatting might not make it across
the Net even though your message will.

E Body or Text: Here's where you type in your message. It can
be short or long.

F Send: When you're finished typing your letter, click here to
send your message.

G Attach Files: Click here in AOL to send a file, such as a document or photo, along with your message. It will open a diaogue
box with a list of your folders and files. Find the file you want
and highlight it. Next click on Attach. Click Done. You'll see the
file listed below the Attachments tab.

91

using an address book

Keep track of friends and family

As you start to receive E-mails from friends and family, it's going to become increasingly difficult to remember all those E-mail addresses. That's why most E-mail programs have an **address book** or **contact** feature to help you keep track of this information. Some programs, like Microsoft's Outlook Express, can store names, multiple phone numbers, several E-mail addresses, as well as several mailing addresses. They can even remember an individual's birthday! America Online, on the other hand, only keeps track of names and E-mail addresses in its address book.

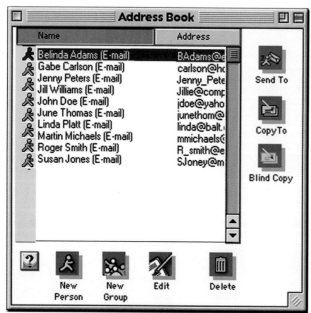

A typical address book lists the E-mail address, as well as any vital particulars you would like to know, such as the person's real name, phone number, address, and birthday.

When you receive an E-mail from a long lost friend, you can add the address to your address book in AOL by clicking on Remember Address. In Microsoft's Outlook Express, click on the Tools menu and select Add Sender to the Contacts option. Now you won't lose track of that person again.

The next time that you want to write a message to someone in your address book, you can select his or her name from a list rather than typing out the entire address.

ASK THE EXPERTS

Can I edit the information in my AOL address book?

When a friend changes E-mail addresses, you can change his information. Open the address book, highlight his name, and click on the Edit button at the bottom of the window.

How can I delete an address book name?

Whether in AOL or any other E-mail program, highlight the name and click on the delete button. In AOL it's at the bottom of the Address Book window. In Outlook Express it's the Delete icon with the trash can at the top of the screen.

In Outlook Express click the New icon to create a new E-mail and then on the Contacts icon at the top of your new message. The Contacts window appears, and you can drag names from the list to the To, CC, or BCC boxes.

now what do I do?

Answers to common problems

Someone wrote 'BFN' in an E-mail to me. What does this mean?

'BFN' means Bye for now. There are many common acronyms used in E-mail because they take up so much less space than writing out the phrase. Here are some others:

BFN	Bye for now	LOL	Laughing out loud
BTW	By the way	TIA	Thanks in advance
FYI	For your information	TTFN	Ta Ta for now

I received an E-mail with an attached file that has .sit after its file name. How do I open it?

You've just gotten a **compressed**, or "stuffed," file. They are much faster to **download,** or copy, from the Internet than a regular unstuffed file. However, to be able to read it, you need to expand it. To do that, you need special software called Stuffit, which you can buy at your local computer store. Or you can download it free from the Web. at **www.macdownloads.com**; first look for Stuffit, then find Stuffit Expander, then select Download now. The program will ask you to save it to your iMac desktop. Once the download is finished, switch to Finder, move to the Desktop, and install the Stuffit Expander by clicking on its **icon,** or picture. The next time you get a .sit file, it will automatically expand into a regular readable file.

What do some of the smiley faces mean in E-mail messages?

The following are a few known **emoticons**, which are "emotions" + "icons:"

:-)	A smile	;-)	A wink
8-)	Goofy smile—or glasses	:-&	Tongue-tied
:-(	Sadness, disapproval	:-p	Tongue stuck out

How can I have my computer tell me when I get an E-mail?

When you are on-line, depending on your E-mail program, new messages might pop up automatically. In AOL, for instance, it will chime "you've got mail" the moment you get a new E-mail. Other programs, such as Outlook Express, require you to set it up. To do so, click on the Preferences button, then click on General Options to reveal Mail and New Settings. Click on Send/Receive and specify how often you wish to be "dinged" when new mail arrives.

How can I forward a message to someone else?

Sometimes when you read an E-mail message, you may want to forward it to another person. For example, you receive a funny joke from your aunt and want your best friend to read it as well. In that case you can forward the message to that person. When you click the Forward button, the message will usually remain at the bottom of the E-mail—unless you have instructed your E-mail not to do that in the preferences area. Then fill out the new-message box just as you would a new message. Try to add a sentence or two that explains why you're forwarding the message.

How can I cut down on spam E-mail?

Most ISP providers have filters that let you screen out unsolicited junk E-mail. For example, on AOL you can just go to the Member Services area and change your options. You can also download Spam Buster or Spammer Slammer for free from download.cnet.com. These programs stop the junk mail from known sources before they clog up your inbox.

I want to send this file to a friend. Will she be able to read it?

Not unless you first translate it into the language that her computer understands. All word processors speak a local dialect, called file formats in computerese, particular to that program. You can send an AppleWorks file to someone who has AppleWorks and he or she will be able to open it. Many word processors (including AppleWorks) have built-in translators to automatically interpret some file formats. Older software, however, often has difficulty reading newer file formats.

If you know your friend's word processor, you can also save the document in a file format her software can read. Click on the File menu and select the Save As option. You'll see a small box under the words Save As. Click and hold down the mouse button on this box and a list of available formats pops up. Your safest bet, however, is to choose the **Rich Text Format,** which acts as a common language among most word processors. It should ensure that your letter arrives with its fonts and indents intact.

 ELPFUL RESOURCES

CONTACTS	BOOKS
America Online www.aol.com 1-888-265-8003	**AOL E-Mail** By Jennifer Watson and Dave Marx
Microsoft www.microsoft.com/mac/ie /default.asp 1-425-882-8080	**The Elements of E-Mail Style: Communicate Effectively Via Electronic Mail** By David Angell
Netscape www.netscape.com/netscape 1-650-254-1900	

Pictures

5

Pictures are worth a thousand words
because they usually cost a bundle.
In this chapter you'll learn how to use free art from the
Internet and pop it into letters. Or use pictures
you've drawn yourself on your computer, or even how
to scan in your own photos.

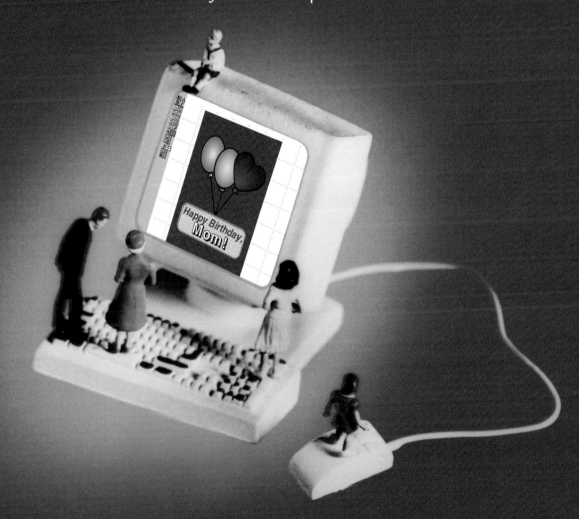

adding pictures

Spice up your letters with an illustration

When a picture is worth a thousand words, why spend hours describing a new home in your holiday letter? A picture or two can show the reader everything you want to get across. And beyond photos, adding illustrations helps break up your text and make it easier—and more fun—to read.

The great thing about adding photos, pictures, or drawings (collectively known as **graphics** to techies) to your documents is that it isn't a big deal. Almost all word processors handle the job with aplomb, and AppleWorks is no exception.

Fortunately, AppleWorks comes with scores of images for you to choose from. These stock images are called **clip art**. See the next page to learn how to insert them.

The picture of a computer shown here can help get your point across or just let you have fun with your correspondence.

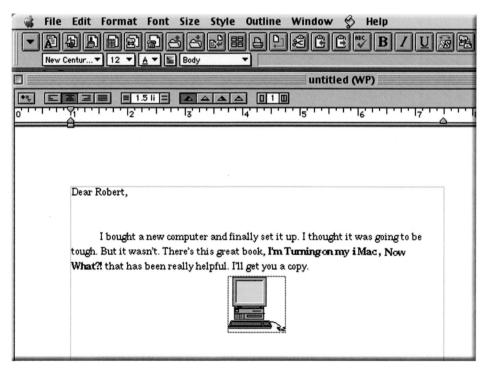

STEP BY STEP: INSERTING A PICTURE

1. To add one of AppleWorks' stock images to a letter you are working on, place your **cursor** at the point where you want to add the image and click. (Remember, the cursor is the I-beam that moves when you pass your mouse over text.) With the letter still on your screen go up to the File menu with your mouse and click on the Library option. You'll see another menu with a long list of libraries. For now, click on the Computer's Library.

2. You'll see a window with a list of names and one image above. Click on each of the names, starting with 3.5" Diskette, to see each image in the Computer's Library. (You can click on the window's View menu and select the By Object option to see all the pictures at once.)

3. To insert the picture shown on the opposite page, click on Computer 3 to select it and click on the Use button. AppleWorks adds the image where you indicated with your cursor.

4. Once the picture has been inserted, close the library's window.

5. To add images other than the clip art, repeat Step 1. But instead of clicking on Library, click on Insert. AppleWorks will display a window that looks a lot like the one for opening a file. Click on the image you want, and AppleWorks inserts it for you.

BLACK AND WHITE OR COLOR?

Just because you've got color on your screen doesn't mean you'll get color when you print. You must have a color printer to see the color that's on your screen. A good ink-jet printer will cost $150 to $250 for the iMac. Just make sure it has a USB connector.

editing pictures

Customize where and how you want your pictures placed

Great. You've found the perfect picture. Now what?
You will probably need to spend a little bit of time making sure your picture looks right. It's easy to both position it and to adjust the size. Here's how.

To adjust the size, click on the clip art to select it. At each of the four corners of the image you will see a little handle. Now click on any one of those handles and drag it with your mouse, pulling it out to make it wider or moving the mouse in to make the image smaller. It's a bit like stretching or shrinking clay.

To move the image, click on it to select it and then drag to wherever you want it. As you move the image to its new location, an outline of the image will move with your mouse pointer, sort of like a traveling footprint. When you release the mouse, the image will be popped into its new place.

Remember this screen shot from page 98? The computer clip art has been resized and moved.

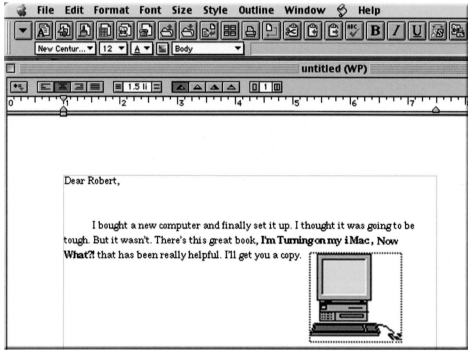

 ## WHAT IF

You want to go back to the original size you started with?

If all your fooling around didn't work and you want to go back to the original size and start all over again, click on one of the handles and hold down the shift key.

You want to move the image to another page in your letter?

Click on the image once to select it. Click on the center of the image (you're in the right spot if your cursor is a silhouette with a box) and drag it to the area where you want it.

You want to get rid of that picture?

Click on the image to select it. Click on the Edit menu and select the Cut option. Voilà. It's gone.

FIRST PERSON DISASTER

Picture Unperfect

It all seemed so easy. My friend E-mailed me the perfect pictures for my art history paper. She said all I had to do was click on the E-mail attachment and they would be ready to put in my report. So I clicked on the icon and got a message asking what program I wanted to open the *vangogh.zip* file with. How should I know? I called my friend and she said the *.zip* meant that the file was compressed to make it quicker to download. She said I needed software to expand it. She said she used Winzip, but it was for PCs and wouldn't work on an iMac. Great. So much for my academic career. A week later I ran into my friend, who said she found out that there was a Macintosh program called Stuffit that could open my file. Too late, I said. I'd already handed in my paper. My teacher marked me down a grade because the paper needed examples of the artist's work.

Jamie C., Poughkeepsie, New York

drawing your own pictures

Create your own greeting cards and other wonders

If you took some time during the last chapter to browse through AppleWorks' libraries of clip art, you saw that they, ahem, lacked virtuosity. You could probably do better, right? Well, now's your chance.

AppleWorks includes both **drawing** and **painting** features. What's the difference between the two? Drawing on a computer is like making a collage. You layer individual pieces on top of one another. You can pull one piece off and leave the rest intact. It's the easiest way to create an image. AppleWorks' painting feature, however, is more like using watercolors or oil paints. Once your "paint" is on the digital canvas, it's there to stay. (One difference from the real world: You can always remove, or undo, the last thing you painted on a computer.) You can also use the painting feature to enhance pictures that you cull from the Web.

AppleWorks' drawing program lets you create your own images or an entire greeting card.

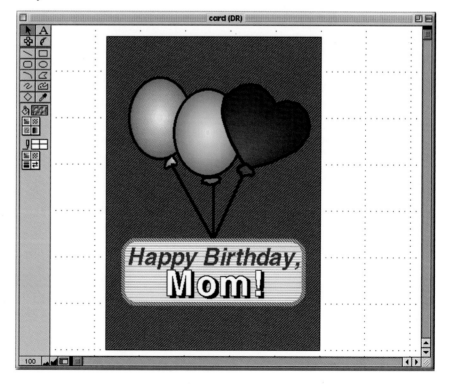

STEP BY STEP: DRAWING PICTURES

1. Click on the File menu and select the New option, which displays the New Document window. Double-click on the Drawing option.

2. You will see a blank sheet, marked off in squares by guidelines (graph paper) with a tool bar on the left side of the window.

3. To get an indication of what each tool does, turn on **Balloon Help** by clicking on the Help menu and selecting Show Balloons. Now you'll see a description of each tool as you move your cursor over its icon on the tool bar.

4. Click on the tool you want to use—Line, Rectangle, Oval, or another choice.

5. Before you click on the canvas and draw the shape you desire, click on a color in the color palette.

6. Create your masterpiece. If you don't like something you've drawn, click on it, and you'll see it surrounded by several dots, which indicate you've selected the item. Click on Edit and then select the Cut option to remove the item. (Hint: To draw a straight line, hold down the Shift key while you drag your line across the digital canvas.)

7. Save your drawing by clicking on the File menu and selecting the Save option. Give it a new name and save it just as you would any other document.

your drawing desktop

AppleWorks' drawing feature includes its own tools as well as those from other
AppleWorks' features. The image at right shows a box for a painting (the banana) within the drawing feature, which lets you see all the graphics tools at one time. It's enough to keep a professional artist busy for an afternoon.

1 Frame Tools—Pointer: First of the four frame tools, the pointer lets you select individual elements in your drawing so you can change their look or eliminate them.

2 Text: Creates a box where you can add text to your drawing. When you start to type with the text tool, notice that the menu options change to include font, size, and style.

3 Spreadsheet: Adds a box where you can add a mini financial spreadsheet to display numbers.

4 Paint: Creates a box within the drawing feature where you can paint a picture (such as the banana).

5 Drawing Tools—Lines: One of the workhorses of the drawing feature that allows you to draw straight lines, squiggly or freehand lines, and curves.

6 Shapes: The favorite graphic tools of non-artists, these tools let you draw perfect rectangles, rounded rectangles, ovals, arcs (a pie slice), and polygons.

7 Painting Tools—Selection: Unlike the drawing itself, a painting doesn't have individual elements that you can pull apart. With the paint feature's rectangle and lasso selection tools, you can select a part of the overall painting to modify or cut.

8 Magic Wand: Allows you to choose all adjacent shades of one color so you can make adjustments.

9 Pencil/Spray Can/Brush: Three painting tools that let you drag a brush across your canvas, spray-paint it, or pinpoint your touch-ups with a pencil. Each tool can be adjusted on the Options menu as long as you've selected the Paint Tool.

10 Paint Bucket: Quickly add paint to a shape that you've created by pouring a bucket onto it.

11 Eraser: Wipe out that monstrosity or deftly remove the rough edges of your work.

12 Eyedropper: Ensures that the color and texture of your next object resembles one you want to mimic. Click on this tool and then an object that you like (say, a box). The next object you create will have the same palette as the original.

13 Paint Palettes: The paint and fill palette controls the color, pattern, texture, and gradient inside a box, oval, or other object.

14 Pen Palettes: The pen palette defines the color, size, and arrows of lines and edges of an object. It also lets you turn lines into arrows.

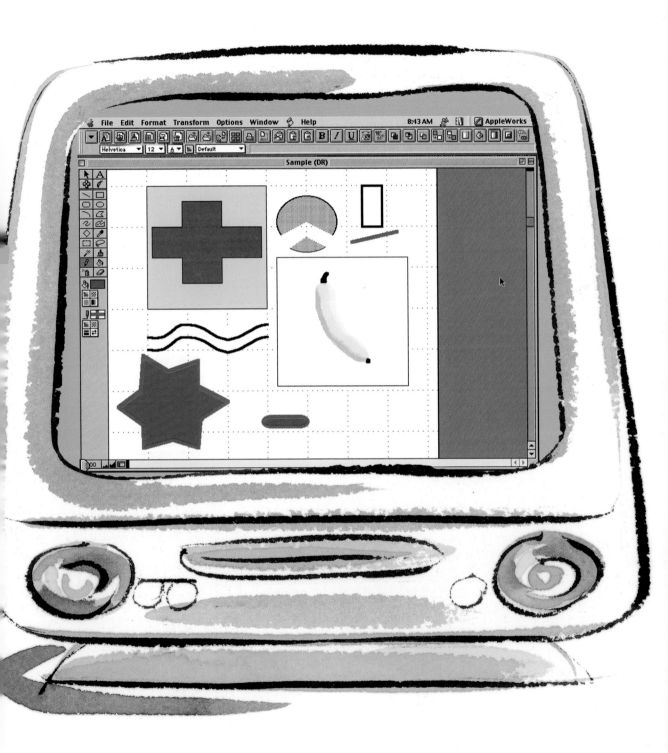

using Web images

Putting pictures from the Web into your documents

Illustrations, photographs, and other graphics are available, many free of charge, from the Web.

It's temptingly easy to get a picture from a Web site, known in techspeak as downloading (see Step by Step at right). Bear in mind, however, that the line between borrowing and stealing is a fine one. Images, just like words in a book, can be copyrighted. Download images from the Web for personal use—say, for a party invitation— and you're fine. But use an Ansel Adams photo of Yosemite on your business flyer, and you could be in trouble.

One site in particular, **www.clipart.com,** acts as a clearinghouse for a number of clip art Web sites.

STEP BY STEP: DOWNLOADING

1. Click on the image that you want to copy and hold down the mouse button.

2. As you keep holding down the mouse button, a small menu will pop down. Select this menu's Download to Disk option, which lets you store the image on your hard drive.

3. You'll now see a Save As window that lets you save a copy of the image wherever you choose on your iMac's hard drive.

4. The next time you're writing a letter in AppleWorks, you can add this image by clicking on File and choosing the Insert option. You can find the image using the Insert window, which looks like an Open File window.

ASK THE EXPERTS

What happens if I get disconnected during the download?

Whether you lose your connection to the Internet or your Web browser stops talking to the image's Web site, you won't have a copy of the image until it successfully completes the download. Get back to that Web site and try it again.

What if I am asked for my credit card number?

Ask yourself if you really need this image for your work. If you're absolutely set on a particular picture, give the site your credit card information only if it's a secure Web site, which you can identify by a Padlock icon at the bottom of your Web browser.

scanning pictures

Use a scanner to put your photographs in your letters

Want to insert pictures of the kids? Your scorecard from the time you broke 100 on the golf course? That adorable smile of your first grandchild? It's easy to do with something called a **scanner,** a device that looks a lot like a home photocopy machine. A scanner will copy your picture electronically, meaning that it converts it into a computer file that you can store in your computer. How exactly is it done? Well, after the image is placed on the scanner surface and the light hits or passes through it, the image is converted into computer code and stored as a digital file in your computer. Computer folk refer to this image as the **scanned image**.

There are many different types of scanners, but **flatbed** scanners are the best for home use and the least expensive. You can buy a scanner at most computer stores. Only look at models that are USB-ready, as you'll have to buy an adapter otherwise. Scanners scan whatever you want, color or black and white. Key point: You can print out a color picture only if you have a color printer; if you have a **monochrome** printer (techspeak for black and white), your color picture will print out in black and white.

Flatbed scanners look like miniature copy machines. Just put your picture face-down, and presto, it's copied into your computer's hard drive.

When you bring your scanner home, you install it the same way you did your printer. You plug it in, hook it up to an empty USB port (or onto the printer's extra USB port), and install its driver software as well as the software application that lets you get images off the scanner. (See page 25 for loading software.)

STEP BY STEP: SCANNING

1. Turn on the scanner.

2. Turn on your computer.

3. Raise the scanner lid, place the image facedown on the glass, and close the lid.

4. Use the scanner software to copy the image. This will include telling the software what type of graphic you're scanning, whether or not it is color, and choosing the resolution. Higher quality images take up more disk space, so a 300 dpi (dots per inch) image file will be smaller than that for a 600 dpi image.

5. Preview your image and, if the preview looks good, scan it.

6. Save the copy of the image to your iMac's hard drive and you can now insert it in an AppleWorks document.

using digital cameras

From the camera to your computer

If you want to have your own photos loaded directly onto your iMac, you should check out digital cameras. You operate these devices just like a regular camera—frame the subject and shoot. The pictures from most new digital cameras are almost indistinguishable from those shot with a traditional camera. The major differences are that you don't have to load film around cogs and you don't have to go to a developer. Actually, you don't have to "develop" the picture at all. How does this amazing invention work? The digital camera stores the photo in its memory. To print the picture or add it to a letter, you attach the camera to your iMac with a USB cable and transfer the pictures to your hard drive. The camera will come with a program that lets you review the images and convert them to a file format you can use in AppleWorks.

The camera lets you determine the quality of the image. Just remember that a higher quality photo takes up more space in the camera's memory. Eventually, however, you will run out of digital "film," which is why you'll need to transfer pictures to your iMac as often as possible.

A nifty feature of most digital cameras is a display of the picture you just took. If you don't like it, reshoot it.

STEP BY STEP: CAMERA TO iMAC

1. First, take your pictures.

2. Plug the camera's USB cable into the camera at one end and your iMac at the other.

3. If you've already loaded your camera's control program, you should now see it start immediately after plugging the camera into the USB port.

4. Wait until the program has loaded previews of the pictures in the camera. Click to select these tiny pictures—called **thumbnails** because they're so small.

5. Click on the Save or Download button (the wording varies depending on which camera you have).

6. Check that the pictures are on your hard drive. Because digital camera software tends to use long strings of numbers as temporary names for your images, you'll want to rename the files to something more memorable.

7. View the file in AppleWorks by clicking on the File menu, selecting the Open option, and then finding your file in the Open window. You can also insert the photo into an existing document by selecting the Insert option from the File menu.

ON-LINE PHOTO DEVELOPMENT

In addition to using scanners and digital cameras to capture photographs electronically, you can also use on-line services to develop your rolls of regular film into digital pictures. Simply take pictures with your regular camera as you normally would. But instead of taking it to the local photo shop, send it to an on-line film developing company. They will process your film, and then the pictures will be scanned and uploaded to a secure area on the Internet accessible by a code given only to you via E-mail. Check out **www.photonet.com** and give it a try. If you're on America Online, check out You've Got Pictures at the keyword Pictures.

now what do I do?

Answers to common problems

When I put pictures in my letters, why do they move around?

You need to lock the photo or image in place. To do so, first you need to display the tool control for AppleWorks' word processor. At the bottom left of your document window you'll see four buttons to the left of the Page indicator. Click on the button immediately to the left of the Page indicator to display the tool control. (Note that there's now no cursor in the document—a necessary condition for adding images that float in place while the text moves around them.) Click on the arrow tool, and then select Insert from the File menu. Once the image is in your letter, choose it by clicking it once and then drag it to a position on the page. Once it's in place, keep the image selected and click on the Options menu and select the Text Wrap option. Choose the Regular or Irregular option, and the text in your document will flow around your photo.

Can I resize my image?

That depends. If you created an object by cobbling together lots of boxes in the Drawing feature, you'll have to change the size of each element—one at a time. If you braved the Painting feature to create your own design, you can resize. Use the paint feature's rectangle selection tool to choose your image. Next, click on the Transform menu and select the Resize feature. Little boxes will appear at the corners of your rectangle selection. Drag one of these corners to adjust the size as you like. Remember, you can always Undo a change if you don't like it.

When I scan my images, where does the software save them?

Most software lets you choose a folder where it will store your images. Some, however, insist on putting all images in their own directories. If you accidentally save a file somewhere without figuring out where it went, don't panic. If the scanning software is still open, click on the File menu and select the Save As option. The Save As window will display the last place you saved a file, and that's where you should go in the Finder to get your file. If you renamed the file, you can also use Sherlock to scan your hard drive for the file by name.

Can I take quality pictures with a consumer digital camera?

It depends on the camera and the quality setting you choose. Most cameras have two or three settings, or resolutions. **Resolution** is a measure of how many dots (also called pixels) appear in the picture. You may have seen the word "megapixel" or 1MP written on the box your camera came in. This means the top quality setting of the camera takes pictures with a million pixels. That's enough to look great when printing out 5"x 7" size photos. You'll need 3MP if you want to print out 8"x10" size photos.

Where can I learn more about digital cameras?

Check out **www.pcphotoreview.com**. You will find product reviews, advice from technical experts, and specifications that will let you compare digital cameras by price and features.

HELPFUL RESOURCES

CONTACTS	BOOKS
Apple Computer www.apple.com/appleworks 1-800-293-6617	**The Non-Designer's Design Book: Design and Typographic Principles for the Visual Novice** By Robin Williams
The Learning Company www.learningco.com 1-617-761-3000	
Adobe www.adobe.com 1-800-833-6687	

e-Finance

6

The whole point of getting a computer is to make your life easier. So start with letting it organize your finances and taxes. How? Read on and find out about various software packages that can help you balance your checkbook and file your taxes. Learn how to use the Internet to shop for a mortgage and keep track of your stocks.

using financial software

*It's already on
your iMac.
Why not try it?*

There is nothing wrong with using good old paper and pencil to track your finances, but what about next year? You have to start all over again, creating the same categories of income and expenses. What if you decide to update your budget during the year? (You do have a budget, don't you?) What if your income increases (wouldn't that be nice) or you switch jobs? If you think it is time to organize your finances—we mean really organize them, not just putting the paid bills in a folder in the filing cabinet—you're going to want to consider getting financial software.

Financial software may be just what you need to keep your bills in order and your budget balanced (or, for that matter, create a budget), and make plans for your financial future.

Yes, you do have to enter all the past and future information about your bank accounts and bills into your computer, but it's there for good (or bad—depending on your spending habits). Once you've added information to your financial software, you're just a few

Quicken, the most popular financial software available, allows you to balance your checkbook, pay bills, and create special lists or graphs for viewing the state of your finances.

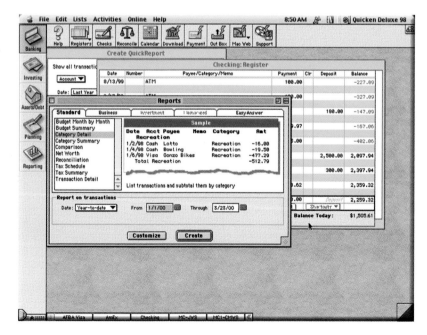

clicks away from connecting it to a tax program (see Using Tax Software in this chapter). And even if you continue using an accountant, financial software organizes all the information that you need to collect for him or her.

You should at least try financial software before rejecting it. After all, Quicken 98—the most popular financial application—came with your iMac. Your only investment will be your time.

SK THE EXPERTS

What's the matter with the budget I wrote in a notebook?

Nothing. In fact, already having a budget is a great start for entering information into Quicken. The advantage of watching your money on the computer is that you can quickly change scenarios should your income change or unexpected expenses land on your doorstep. It's also great at helping you determine your net worth and plan for retirement.

How often should I update my information with new checks that I've written and expenses that I've made?

That's up to you, but most people do not do so daily, or even weekly. Updating Quicken when you pay your monthly bills will work fine.

How can I protect my financial information from snoopers?

The greatest risk to the privacy of your information comes not from Internet **hackers** (usually computer whiz kids who like to see if they can break computer security codes), but from friends or relatives who share your home computer. Quicken lets you protect your financial files by using a password. After you've entered your information, click on the Edit menu and select the Preferences option. On the list of various settings, scroll down until you can click on the Passwords option and type in a password to open the file. It's a good idea to use a password if you are sharing your iMac with a lot of folks. Otherwise it's not necessary if it's your personal home computer.

QUICKEN ON-LINE

Intuit, the publisher of Quicken, aggressively expanded the product's features in recent years with links to the Internet. In the coming sections you'll see that Quicken can connect you to your bank as well as to on-line stock quotes to keep your portfolio up-to-date. The program can even retrieve electronic copies of your bank or investment statements, eliminating tedious input on your part.

financial Web sites

Top-drawer financial information is just a click away

The Web now contains such a vast amount of information it's a virtual library in space. To speed your search through it you need a librarian. In computerland, librarians are called search engines. You might have heard of some of them, Excite or Yahoo! for example. These search engines look through the whole Web for you, and bring to your computer screen only what you requested, for example, international mutual funds. However, because financial information is so popular, most search engines have created mini search engines just for finance and money. Ergo, instead of searching through all of Yahoo! for information on mutual funds, go right to their finance section. How do you do that? Go to your Web address bar and type in finance.yahoo.com. Here are some of the financial sections within popular search engines you should check out(you don't need www.):

> **quicken.excite.com**
>
> **finance.yahoo.com**
>
> **moneycentral.msn.com**
>
> **personalfinance.netscape.com**

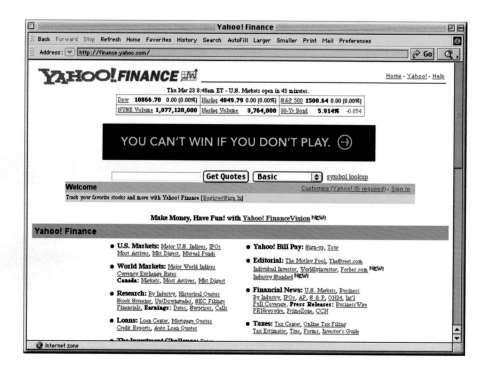

ASK THE EXPERTS

Can I find the latest investment research on-line?

If you're serious about investing, there's no reason to ask your broker to send reports on a particular company or mutual fund. They're available on-line. Two favorite sites where you can find information on thousands of stocks, mutual funds, bonds, and more, are:

www. morningstar.com

www.zwss.com

What are these calculators that I see on some sites?

Many Web sites include forms that help you determine everything from the size of the mortgage you can afford to the amount of money you need to stash away each year to meet your long-term financial goals. The computer that hosts the Web site calculates the numbers from information you provide and presents an answer tailored to your situation. You can find several useful calculators at **www.kiplinger.com** and **www.bloomberg.com**.

Can Web sites help me figure out foreign currency?

If you're looking at Web sites for an upcoming vacation overseas, you'll want to convert the quoted rates into dollars so you can budget accurately. You need to steer your Web browser to the Universal Currency Converter located at **www.xe.net/currency**.

When you go there, put the amount to convert in the box at left and then locate the currency you're converting from in the left-hand list. This can be confusing at first, because the site sorts currency alphabetically by country, not the three-digit bank codes that precede each country's name. Once you've found the currency, click on it, then pick USD (U.S. Dollars) in the right-hand column. Click the Perform Currency Conversion button, and you're taken to a page that gives you the exact dollar amount.

ALL FINANCE, ALL THE TIME

Sometimes following the market becomes an obsession. When that urge hits, turn to on-line news sources. Some key locations for round-the-clock coverage:

www.cnbc.com
Information as it breaks from one of the leading financial cable channels.

www.cnnfn.com
Hot stories about business, the economy, and politics from Ted Turner's financial baby.

www.marketwatch. com
CBS News's site for tracking the day's financial events.

www.thestreet.com
A major source of independent financial news on the Web.

www.fool.com
The Motley Fool provides up-to-date info and down-to-earth advice.

banking on-line

You may never have to walk into a bank again

Banking is one of the greatest hassles we face on a regular basis. Who looks forward to balancing the checkbook and correcting errors? (You do balance your checkbook every month, don't you?) On-line banking, combined with the use of Quicken, simplifies the process. It allows you to keep your checkbook balanced with a minimum effort, and lets you see whether checks have cleared before your monthly statement shows up in the mail or how quickly a deposit becomes available. In fact, Quicken can connect directly to most banks' computers and retrieve data automatically.

How safe is on-line banking? Banks are very conservative and understand your concerns over access to account information. The banks have installed **fire walls** (rugged computer programs that ensure their systems are used only by known customers). They've also password-protected your account, so they can verify that you should be allowed access, but no one else. For further protection, information flying to your browser from the bank is **encrypted** (techspeak for a secret code that crooks can't break). Also, just as you would with an ATM transaction, you must provide a personal identification number, or PIN, for each transaction.

The Gomez Web site is the place to go to locate information about on-line banking services across the country.

If this sounds worth investigating, you can call your bank to find out if they currently offer on-line banking. You can also use Quicken's Help feature to browse through a list of contact information for several big and small banks (or go on-line to **www.quicken.com** to find an updated list of banks offering these services). Click on the Help feature's Topic option, select the On-line Banking topic, and click on the phrase "How do I set up on-line banking?"

If your bank lacks on-line banking and that's the final straw in your dissatisfaction with it, you can investigate banks offering on-line banking at **www.gomez.com** or **www.cyberinvest.com**. They even rate some banks that have no branches and exist only on the Web.

ASK THE EXPERTS

How are monthly fees charged?

Although many banks provide basic on-line banking for free, most will charge for extra services. Your bank will automatically deduct any fees from your checking account.

How do I deposit money into my account?

Your bank can provide postage-paid, addressed envelopes for mailing deposits directly to the institution. Of course, your employer (and the Social Security Administration) can deposit money directly into your account so you won't need to go to the bank. And finally, you can always deposit checks at your ATM.

How do I get cash?

Print your own bills, and folks from the Treasury Department will pay you a visit. The only way to get cash is to rely on ATMs and branch offices, just as you always have. If you use an on-line-only bank, ATMs are the only place you can get cash. The only difference is that when you take out your money, it will immediately be posted to your on-line account.

TO ERR IS HUMAN

Banks make mistakes—even when they're technologically up-to-date. If you decide to use electronic banking, you still need to reconcile your bank's reckoning of your account with your own records. If you find a mistake, contact the bank immediately to find out what steps need to be taken to correct the error.

paying bills on-line

Never get late payment fees again

Paying bills is always painful, but you can simplify it with your iMac, browser, and Internet connection. New on-line services from most banks and companies such as Intuit let you pay bills on-line. Although many of these services charge you to pay bills (usually around $7 per month), the cost is generally worth it. First off, you save the cost of a stamp for each payment. Make more than 20 payments in a month, and the service pays for itself in postage.

These companies pay your bills with two methods of electronic payment. Some have arranged to pay them electronically to your creditors. They wire your payment directly to the account of the utility company, for instance. If your creditor does not accept electronic payments, the payment company sends a paper check to pay the bill. If you owe a friend some money for a share of a group vacation, for example, you can instruct your on-line bill payer to send a check to your friend. You could just write your own checks, of course, but then you'd miss out on seeing those payments on the various reports that these firms offer to track your expenses.

Some of these programs, especially from banks, include special software, but more frequently they require a Web browser and a connection to the Internet. The special applications often are unavailable for Macintosh, but banks increasingly recognize Apple's resurgence, so they now support Quicken on the Mac. Unfortunately, you need to make sure that you've got the right version—it might require the newer Quicken 2000 rather than the Quicken 98 that shipped with the iMac until early 2000. Some banks will also charge you to pay bills via Quicken, even though they'll charge you nothing if you use a Web browser. Go figure.

SK THE EXPERTS

What are the benefits of on-line bill paying?

Primarily, you're avoiding writing a check as well as stuffing and mailing an envelope. But you'll also gain the ability to create reports of payments and the ability to import the payment information directly to Quicken so they get reflected in your budget.

How long does it take for payees to receive payment?

It's not instant, that's for sure. Electronic payments take at least 3 days to be received and processed by your creditor. Your creditors receive paper check payments in 5 to 7 days. So don't expect on-line payments to bail you out from being late at the last minute. You can anticipate forgetfulness by setting up payments to be made automatically on a specific date.

How do I know which companies accept on-line checks?

Call their customer service number and ask. If they do, ask how to sign up. Some companies require written notification that you will be sending on-line checks to them via your E-mail; others let you set it up right over the phone.

How can I stop an on-line check?

If you need to stop payment on an on-line check, know there will be penalties just as if it were a paper check. If the on-line check hasn't been cashed yet, you may be able to cancel it on-line. Most likely you will have to call the company and explain the problem.

PAYING BILLS BY PHONE

Some companies are still stuck in the 1980s technologically. They're incapable of accepting on-line payment but will let you pay bills by phone. Generally you give them your bank routing number, bank account number, the payment amount, and a specific check number (if it's a checking account). The routing, check, and account numbers are on the bottom left of each of your checks. The following month (or next time you have a payment), call them with the amount of the bill and a new check number. They'll deduct the amount directly from your checking account, and it will show up on your next bank statement.

shopping for a mortgage

Getting approved (or, ahem, declined) on-line

In the old days you called your bank to see if it would, please, maybe, give you a loan. It told you the interest rate. You shrugged and gladly accepted the offer. With the Internet you can kiss your subservience good-bye. Among the places to turn when you need a mortgage:

www.eloan.com Offers prequalification and preapproval for home-equity loans, first mortgages, and refinancing. Check your loan status on-line as well as compare the values of neighborhood homes. This site will E-mail you when a particular interest rate becomes available.

www.homeadvisor.msn.com Features 11 lenders, but has an easy-to-use, 10-step application process and helpful work sheets.

Need to keep abreast of interest rates as you move to closing? Check out www.bankrate.com and www.banxquote.com.

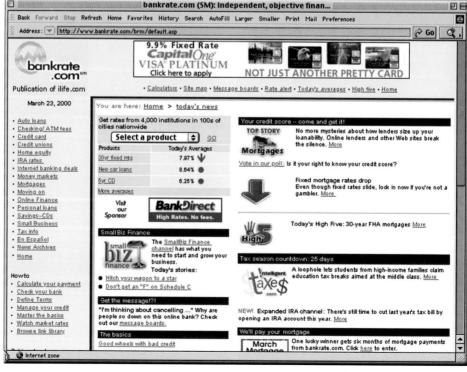

www.mortgagelocator.com Allows you to type in your rate and terms, and interested lenders contact you. You can also chat on-line directly with lenders and real estate agents (see "Chatting On-line" if you don't know how to do this).

www.quickenmortgage.com Requires you to answer a lot of personal questions to prequalify for a loan. When you finish, though, you'll get a list of possible loans that you can apply for instantly.

HAT IF

You want to find a house, but you don't know where to look?

The real estate industry has taken to the Web as the best way to disseminate information about homes to as many potential purchasers as possible. You can scope out the housing market at the following sites:

www.cyberhomes.com Provides interactive street-level mapping and an E-mail service that notifies you anytime someone lists a home that fits your criteria.

www.realtor.com The home of the National Association of Realtors contains more than a million homes nationwide. You can also investigate crime statistics for a neighborhood and the quality of the local schools.

www.homeseekers.com Lists more than 650,000 homes nationwide and is updated daily.

www.homebuilder.com When you're only interested in new homes, this site lists more than 125,000 properties and can line you up with custom builders who can help you create your own castle.

KEEPING CURRENT

For objective data on interest rates and terms from a site that doesn't make loans or accept lender advertising, take a look at **www.hsh.com**. This site just surveys lenders—2500 across the country—and updates quoted rates daily.

using tax software

Tax software helps ease the pain of filing

Few things put people on edge like trying to file their own taxes. No wonder millions turn to accountants each year for help in preparing their returns.

The two primary tax applications for the Macintosh are MacInTax and Kiplinger Tax Cut. Both software programs include interview features that ask questions and explain each step in plain English. As you fill in responses, the application pulls together your tax return. Each also includes the latest changes to the tax code. They incorporate much of the advice that you'd normally seek from an accountant—just a click away on the Help feature.

This is not a fast process. Plan on setting aside several hours one weekend to complete the interview. Once you're done, the applications let you compare yourself to an average U.S. taxpayer in your income bracket. They also provide advice on how to reduce taxes in the years ahead.

MacInTax includes video clips that illustrate complex tax concepts in plain English. If you have trouble hearing tax lady, your computer's sound level may be too low. Turn up the volume by clicking on your control panel and then selecting sound. You should see a volume control feature you can adjust with your mouse.

HAT IF

You've been using Quicken all year to track and categorize your expenses?

Then MacInTax is the product you should use. It's created by Intuit, the same company that makes Quicken, and can grab data directly from your Quicken files, speeding up your tax preparation.

You want to download IRS forms?

The CD-ROMs of most tax applications include the forms you need to fill out your taxes. Sometimes, however, you need an updated form or the disk is missing information on an obscure part of the tax code. You also might need a special state tax form. You can download any IRS form or instruction from **www.irs.gov**, which also has links to the forms for state revenue agencies. Choose either the Electronic Services or Forms & Pubs link.

You want to file your taxes on-line?

Filing on-line gets your refund back to you fast. Most tax preparation software includes information on how to file on-line. However, not all states accept electronic filing. Call your local state tax office to see if yours does.

You can also prepare your return on-line at **www.turbotax.com** (also owned by Intuit) without buying its tax software. This Web version of TurboTax charges you $9.95 to file a federal return and another $9.95 to file one for your state. You can pause in the middle of completing the interview and return a day or so later (you just need to log back in with your password). The on-line program provides you with a copy of your return in Adobe's Portable Document Format (or PDF), which you can print out just as if it were from MacInTax.

on-line investing

Trading securities and mutual funds on-line

You can now purchase stocks, bonds, and mutual funds over the Internet. These **on-line brokers** charge substantially less than a traditional broker to buy or sell an investment. The extremely discounted fees can run as low as $7 per trade. The downside? You're on your own for researching which stock, bond, or fund to buy. Fortunately, on-line brokerages (as well as sites such as **cnnfn.com**) include scads of data on companies and funds. They've also got discussion groups where individual investors gather to discuss the market and share tips. Always beware chat-room stock advice.

Happy with your current broker? In response to the growth of on-line investment sites, almost every traditional brokerage has developed a way for individuals to buy stocks on-line at a discount. Ask your broker about these options. Otherwise, consider looking into one of these on-line brokerages:

www.ameritrade.com   **www.fidelity.com**
www.schwab.com   **www.etrade.com**

To trade at these sites, you have to set up an account—a process similar to setting up an on-line banking account. The brokerage will verify your information and then send you several forms by U.S. mail for you to sign and return along with a payment for an initial deposit. The brokerage then sends back your user I.D. and password so you can go to the site, log on, and start trading.

On-line brokerages put you in control of investment decisions and charge low prices for buying and selling stocks, bonds, and mutual funds.

ASK THE EXPERTS

What should I look for in an on-line brokerage?

Poke around their site to see what research they have (and whether they charge a premium to access it) and their fee structure (which should be clearly defined). Also try contacting them by phone to get some sense of how they respond should you be unable to get through to their Web site for any reason.

What are day traders?

Day traders are speculators. They buy and sell stocks rapidly, hoping to make a profit on price swings. The advent of on-line trading has enabled many people to speculate from home—or try to make a living at it in an office. Few day traders, however, actually make money because they usually don't quit when they are ahead.

FIRST PERSON DISASTER

On-line Trading Addiction

I feel like I could go on Oprah or something: The mom who became a Day Trader Junkie. It started out innocently enough. All I wanted to do was be able to keep a better eye on my stocks so I signed up with an E-trade outfit that gives you instant updates on the stock market. It was so easy to get an E account, and after one week I made my first trade on-line. I felt very hip. Now all I feel is exhausted. The problem is that it's so easy to check your stocks any time of day or night, that any sudden market move can drive you nuts. Guess what? Sometimes the market shifts every five minutes. There were days when I never left the house. All I did was watch my E-trade account. It got so bad that I missed my daughter's tennis tournament. She came home sobbing because I wasn't there. I knew then and there it was time to call it quits. I transferred my whole E account to a broker. Let him worry about it for me.

Mimi K., Morristown, New Jersey

now what do I do?

Answers to common problems

Why isn't my financial software displaying its video features?

When you install most software applications that have videos (including finance and tax software, encyclopedias, and games), the videos aren't added to your hard drive. They're still on the CD-ROM to save hard drive space. To view the video, make sure the disk is in your CD-ROM player.

What is priceline.com and how do I use it?

Priceline is an on-line service (**www.priceline.com**) that lets you bid on items such as airfares, hotel rooms, mortgages, and groceries. You choose an amount that you're willing to pay, and Priceline sees whether any company is willing to accept that price or (in the case of mortgages) rate. In other words, Priceline eliminates the list price and lets you haggle for a lower one.

How can I increase my Web browser security?

Most browsers provide varying levels of security. Click on your browser's Preference option—in America Online, it's on the My AOL menu. Click on Security (in AOL, you'll need to take the extra step of clicking on the WWW icon and selecting Advanced Settings), and you'll be able to adjust the security level (called Security Zones in Internet Explorer and AOL). More is generally better, but the highest level of security may prevent you from working properly with certain financial Web sites.

Can hackers eavesdrop on my visits to an on-line bank?

The latest browsers include a security procedure that prevents anyone from tapping your computer's conversation with your on-line bank. The bottom of your browser should indicate that this is a "secure" connection. If the link isn't secure, you aren't protected. It's a good idea to check a bank's security procedures before signing up for their on-line banking service.

Where can I find out more about filing taxes electronically?

Straight from the IRS. The agency lets you **e-file**, as the government techies call it, three different ways. You can have a tax professional do it for you, file it yourself via the Internet with tax preparation software, or use a touch-tone phone to dial in the simplest returns. You can **download** (copy) IRS publication 1857 from **www.irs.gov** to read about each of these options. Just click on the site's Electronic Services, then click on IRS e-file for individuals, then click on publication 1857.

How can I read the documents that I download from the IRS site?

All government agencies electronically publish their documents in Adobe's Portable Document Format, or PDF. Adobe distributes the free Acrobat Reader program to view these items, and Apple installed it on your iMac before shipping it out of the factory. You should be able to double-click on the file and view it in Acrobat. If not, go to the Apple Extras folder on your hard drive and you'll find an Acrobat folder from which you can install the application.

Can Quicken help me remember bill payment dates?

Absolutely! Quicken lets you set up reminders that alert you to upcoming payments. First, however, you need to set up a list of payments that you plan on making in the future, including such monthly bills as mortgage or rent. Click on the Calendar icon and select the New Transaction. Make the payment recurring by selecting a Frequency and then tell the calendar how many days in advance to notify you of future transactions.

 HELPFUL RESOURCES

CONTACTS	BOOKS
Intuit www.quicken.com 1-650-944-6000	**The 9 Steps to Financial Freedom** By Suze Orman
Block Financial Corp. www.taxcut.com 1-818-779-7223	**The Wall Street Journal Guide to Understanding Money & Investing** By Kenneth M. Morris, Virginia B. Morris, and Alan M. Siegel
	Personal Finance for Dummies (2nd Ed) By Eric Tyson

e-Genealogy

7

Getting back to your roots was never so easy as with a computer. In this chapter you'll learn how to use the Internet and the various software packages out there to research your family history and pull it together into a real family tree. It's as easy as pie—make that grandma's apple pie.

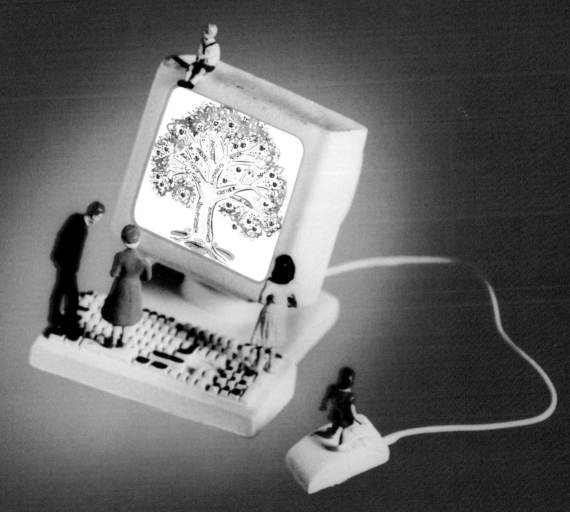

genealogy Web sites

Tapping on-line databases for information on your relatives

Collecting all the names, dates, and places that your family can remember may only whet your appetite. Why not turn to the Internet to push your search back further. To get an idea of all the resources waiting for you, try the two leading free sites:

www.genealogy.com Here you can search for missing family links, although some of the links lead to sales pitches for CD-ROM products that mention your ancestors. (Unfortunately, many of these disks are for Windows only.) Click on the Classes link on the home page and you'll find a lengthy list of topics covered by Genealogy.com experts.

www.cyndislist.com Whether you need a lesson about how to hunt through adoption records or assistance continuing your search in another country, Cyndi's List can help you find useful resources. Unlike Genealogy.com, the site doesn't provide a searchable database of ancestors but links you to several free and commercial sites where you can hunt for information. Don't expect quick answers. Many of the links just include information that requires you write to a source requesting information.

Genealogists quickly adopted the Web to connect with other researchers, publish their findings, and provide tips for other investigators. That's why you can find everything on the Web from discussion boards to family histories to genealogical primers.

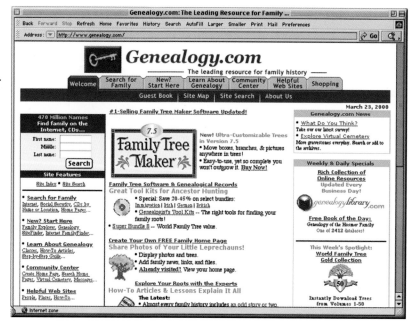

ASK THE EXPERTS

What's the best way to get started?

There are so many resources on-line that you'll do best by setting aside an evening to click through an on-line class at Cyndi's List. The course will help you understand what information will be most helpful for your search. For instance, if you know your relative was in the armed forces, you'll learn about various sources of military information.

Will I really have to spend years conducting research?

Family trees become more extensive and obscure the further back in time you go. To trace all these nooks and crannies, most genealogists passionately pursue their avocation over several years. Don't have the time to devote to a lengthy search? You can always hire a professional to do the work for you. Genealogical Web portals have links to these pros, but beware. Hired researchers will never be the sticklers for accuracy that you will be in tracing your own family.

genealogy software

Sure the Web is a great place to mosey around to find your past, but there's plenty of software that offers more information, tools, and features than these genealogy Web sites. And once you've paid for the software, which usually ranges in price from $50 to $80, you have access to the hundreds of thousands of names that come with the program.

How do these programs manage to deliver all of this information? Simple. Along with the software, you get several CD-ROMs (disks with information on them). You load these CDs one by one on your CD-ROM drive (see page 24). Some genealogy software comes with lots of CDs. Do yourself a favor and buy a CD-ROM rack for your software shelf for easy access.

The genealogy software is far friendlier and easier to use than the genealogy Web sites because navigating from one section to another is easier. Always read the interactive multimedia tutorials in each of the programs before you begin. Although building a family tree is easy, you can get confused if you jump right in and enter names and dates without understanding where everything goes. You don't want to have to reenter your family information because you mistakenly "married" your newborn granddaughter to your long deceased great-grandfather.

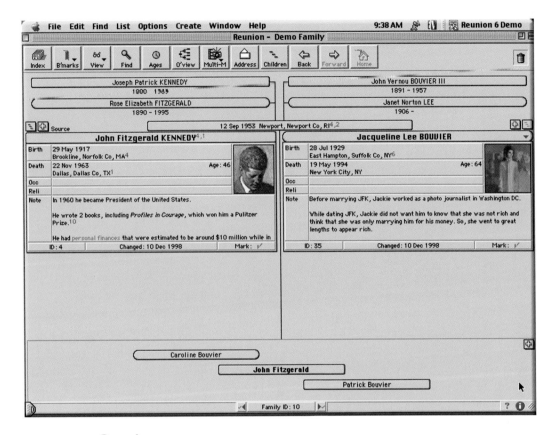

Reunion

With the ability to add pictures and a place for the most intricate details (including the family pet), Reunion uses the point-and-click Macintosh interface to its fullest. You can add scanned images of your ancestors and even movies from a family reunion. You begin by recording information about your family, but you can import information from other programs, as well.

more genealogy software

Family Tree Maker

Although it remains the champion of the Microsoft Windows universe, the Macintosh version of Broderbund's Family Tree Maker isn't quite as slick as Reunion. Still, it comes with a CD-ROM set that includes four disks containing Social Security records from 1937 to 1996. You can also import records from thousands of Family Tree users who've sent their family information to Broderbund to share with other researchers.

ASK THE EXPERTS

I want to get data from my cousin who's been using a Windows program.

Just as word processors, spreadsheets, databases, and graphics programs have common file formats that work for their programs, so do genealogy programs. Ask your cousin to save all the research in GED-COM files (see page 140), which you can receive by E-mail and import to your program.

What is shareware or freeware and how do I get it?

Genealogy attracts passionate part-time software developers who devise programs, because it marries their programming skills to their hobby. They usually distribute these applications as shareware or freeware—programs that you can download from the Internet for free. Developers don't charge you for freeware and generally put you on the honor system to send in payment for shareware applications. (Some developers limit shareware's features unless you pay them for the program.)

Apple lists commercial software, shareware, and freeware at **apple.com/software**. There you'll find information on the genealogy shareware program Gene and the freeware application Bygones.

FIRST PERSON DISASTER

Software Gone Soft

I gave my husband this incredible genealogy software package for his birthday. He couldn't wait to try it. He put it on the CD-ROM drive and waited for the software picture to appear on our computer desktop. All he got was an obscure error message. He tried loading it again. Same error message. I could feel my blood pressure rising. The computer was only a few months old and already it was broken. Then I had the bright idea to call the software maker and find out what was wrong. I found the number on the back of the box and called. After a few minutes on hold I got a real person and told him our problem. "Oh, yeah, there was a problem with one of the batches of CDs that went out. Sorry. If you give me your address I'll mail you a replacement." I was so relieved there wasn't something seriously wrong with our computer that I wasn't even mad at their sloppy quality control.

Roberta T., San Diego, California

on-line research

Using the Web for genealogy's heavy lifting

The Web also contains database lists full of raw information about your ancestors. You just might not know where to look. You'll find two main sources when you begin poking around. Another big source comes from databases of families, generally compiled in GEDCOM files submitted by individual researchers. (The GEDCOM file format was created by the Church of Jesus Christ of Latter-day Saints (the Mormons) to make tracking names easier.) Here are some places you'll want to return to often in your search:

www.familysearch.com The entire database of the Church of Jesus Christ of Latter-day Saints is on-line.

www.rootsweb.com RootsWeb is the public broadcaster of Web-based genealogical research. You can tap its databases for free, or send in a check to support its not-for-profit efforts. Visit the site, and you'll find more than 23 million potential relatives on file.

On-line databases of families let you piggyback on the work of other re-searchers to zero in on the lineage of specific ancestors.

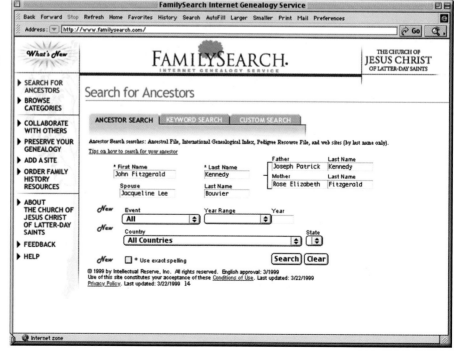

www.genexchange.com You'll be connected to free on-line records subdivided by state and county to help narrow your search. Tap these piles of data, and you may turn up the wedding date of a distant relative or a parcel of land they purchased.

www.usgenweb.com Similar to the GenExchange, USGenWeb is attempting to bring more free documents on-line. Among its several ongoing projects: providing digital maps of U.S. counties and the Tombstone Project, which asks members to post their surveys of old graveyards.

 SK THE EXPERTS

Why aren't my ancestors in a database?

Few things are as gratifying as finding a long-dead relative in an on-line database and being able to click back through your ancestry from child to parent. But it doesn't always work that way. Genealogy requires someone researching information. On-line databases require someone submitting data. When neither of these things happen, there's not much chance you'll find your ancestors on-line. Maybe you should appoint yourself chief family researcher and add the material you find to the growing body of genealogical knowledge on the Web.

Why aren't all the records available on-line?

Very few old documents have been transcribed for computer access. More often they're sitting in dusty files waiting for you to find them. Several volunteer projects seek to bring these files on-line. Consider volunteering your spare time. If you're already transcribing your great-great-grandfather's name from the list of a ship's manifest, consider copying down the entire list and submitting it to an on-line ship-registry site.

spreading the family tree

Create a visual expression of your family

Ever attend a family reunion or wedding only to find yourself trying to remember who's the child of whom? Was Cousin Ellen the daughter of Uncle Bill? Or did you hear that she was a first cousin twice removed, whatever that is?

These and other quandaries can be avoided by printing a family tree. Most genealogy software lets you print your family data in several tidy formats. But first you need to know the basic charts used in genealogy:

Ancestor Chart—Also known as Pedigree chart, the ancestor chart is the greatest boon ever for a neglected child. It puts you at the center of the family. All the marriages lead inevitably to the blessed moment when you came on the planet. Yours is the only birth that matters. Sure, it's a little bit simplified with siblings and cousins excluded, but it's an easy way to show the kids their grandparents and all the greats that preceded them.

Descendant Chart—An ancestor takes center stage so you can show all his or her descendants. Because everyone can trace their connections through the family tree, distant cousins can use this to introduce themselves at a family reunion. Descendant charts can often be expanded by creating a relative chart that shows your ancestor's ancestors as well as his or her descendants.

A chart of your family tree makes a great gift for a family get-together.

STEP BY STEP: A FAMILY TREE

1. Add the family facts that you know.

2. Select the type of chart you want to display. In Family Tree Maker you click on View and choose the chart type from the pull-down list. In Reunion you click on Create and select the appropriate chart.

3. Tell the program the number of generations that you want to go back for ancestors and forward for descendants. (In Family Tree Maker you need to adjust this setting on the Contents menu.)

4. In Reunion you'll need to click on the Chart button to create the chart (Family Tree Maker automatically generates it).

5. Click on the File menu and select the Print option.

now what do I do?

Answers to common problems

What can I add to make my family tree look nicer?

With most genealogy software you can spruce up a chart or a database with pictures from your family's past. To add a photo, you first need to scan the image (see the "Pictures" chapter). Once the scanner software has turned the picture into a file on your hard drive, you can follow the genealogy program's directions to add it to your database.

I don't have a scanner. How can I get my photos inserted?

Try contacting a local copy or graphics shop. They have scanners and computers and for a fee will scan in your photos and give them to you on a computer disk that you can then load into your computer at home. They can also edit your photos (get out all those red eyes from the flashbulb). They can "stitch" together ripped photographs too.

When I scan old family photos, will I damage them?

Scanning doesn't hurt old photos. It actually can help preserve them by capturing a digital image that won't change over time. You can even touch up cracked or torn old photos in AppleWorks' Paint feature.

How long does it take to create a family tree?

How long do you have? Even if you have to place a few calls to siblings or parents, you should be able to create a simple three-generation tree (you, your parents, and your grandparents) in an afternoon. The further back you go and the more extensive your chart becomes, the longer it takes.

Should I worry about adding my family's name to a Web site?

You should post information only to sites that detail their privacy policies on the Web. If you don't like what the site says it will do with your information, don't submit it there. The safest sites should provide password protection and promise not to sell your data to marketing companies. Never add Social Security information to the Web and always remove any living relatives' information if they request you to do so.

Can I E-mail the family tree to family members?

Absolutely, but chances are they won't be able to open the file unless they have the same genealogy software program as you. You can always save your information as a GEDCOM file, which most family tree programs can work with. How do you do this? On the file menu of Reunion or Family Tree Maker, select the Export feature and choose GEDCOM as the file format in which you want to write the information.

But why force them through all that work?

Most programs let you post your work to the Web, where any on-line family member can view your work without a special genealogy program. One unpredictable benefit may be that distant relatives will see the work on-line and contact you out of the blue with more information to help fill out your tree.

How can other family members contribute to my tree?

Ask them to send you any family memories, anecdotes, photos, and even films. As you add these elements to your site, you'll develop a rich family archive. Who knows? Thanks to your work, the family may decide that it's time for a reunion.

ELPFUL RESOURCES

CONTACTS	BOOKS
Broderbund (Family Tree Maker) www.broderbund.com 1-617-761-3000	**How to Trace Your Family Tree: A Complete and Easy to Understand Guide for the Beginner** By American Genealogical Research Institute
Leister Productions, Inc. (Reunion) www.leisterpro.com 1-800-800-2222	**Beginners Ancestor Research Kit** By Philip Beck
	The Unpuzzling Your Past Workbook: Essential Forms and Letters for All Genealogists (1st Edition) By Emily Anne Croom

e-Travel

8

He won't ask for directions;
she won't look at a map. Thanks to the computer,
this age-old dilemma has been solved.
In this chapter you'll see how simple it is to go on-
line and get instant directions for exactly
where you want to go or how to use
various trip-planning software packages.

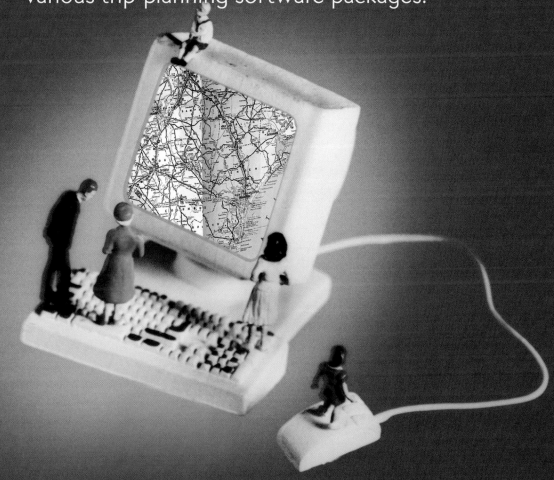

planning a trip

Throw away those old maps

Why would you ever need your iMac to plan a trip?
After all, you can just as easily pull out maps and locate all the information you need for a trip across town or cross-country.

Ah, it may not be portable, but your iMac is powerful and provides certain advantages over maps. First, **computer mapping software** contains several layers of detail. You can view a city at the simplistic level of the maps given out at rental-car counters. Or you can zoom down to the block of your final destination—whether it's a hotel or a friend's home.

Computer maps also know about those obscure state parks and roadside attractions. But by far the best reason to plan a trip with your computer is that it can plot a route from Point A to Point B— even crossing state lines or the entire continent. (Try that with several state maps sprawled out before you.) Your iMac becomes a mini AAA, waiting at your beck and call to produce a customized TripTik.

You've got two options for plotting a trip on your iMac. You can turn to the Web (see "Using the Web to Plan Your Trip" in this chapter), or buy Street Atlas USA—the primary trip planning CD-ROM for the Macintosh. The Web sites are free, but waiting for a map to load can take minutes over a slow modem connection. Priced less than $50, the CD-ROM includes a wealth of information and loads in a jiffy.

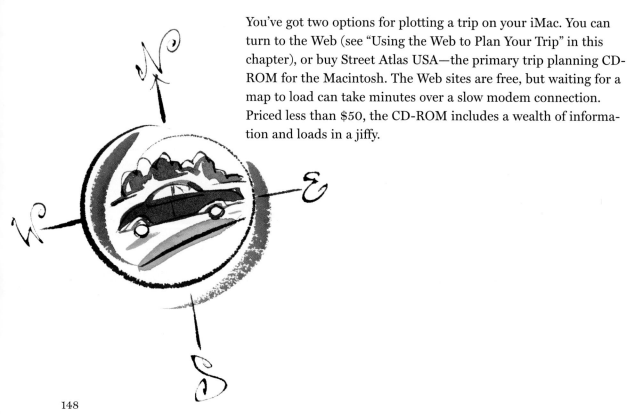

File Edit Find View Plan Route GPS Help   9:52 AM   Street Atlas USA 6.0

DeLorme Street Atlas USA 6.0 - startup

Start: Cold Spring, NY   Finish: Katonah, NY

Preferred Route
Trip distance is 28.1 mi
Trip time is 0:43

Road	Leg	Time	Dist	Dir
Start - Cold Spring, NY				
SR 9D (Chestnut St|Scen...	8.6	0:00	0	S
US 6 (US 202|Highland ...	3.8	0:12	9	SE
Bear Mountain State Pkwy	5.8	0:17	12	E
US 202 (SR 35|Crompo...	4.7	0:26	18	E
SR 35 (Amawalk Rd)	4.8	0:33	23	E
Woodsbridge Rd	0.5	0:41	28	S
Finish - Katonah, NY		0:43	28	

magnitude 11   2 miles

Street Atlas USA Trying to map your route the night before a big trip may prove frustrating if you've never used Street Atlas USA before. You can teach yourself how to use the product by trying a simple test. After you load the software (see page 25), try mapping the route from your home to a friend or family member's house several miles away. You'll learn how to use the product by noting how its features display familiar locations. This software also displays a map detailing the route between the two points, which you can print and take with you. Better still, it gives turn-by-turn directions that will prevent your getting lost on the journey. Check out the total mileage for the trip as well as the expected driving time. Now you won't be late for Aunt Mildred's pot roast dinner!

using the Web to plan a trip

Let these Web sites tell you where to go

Terrific directions for your next business or family trip are as close as your Web browser, and they're free (although they do come with advertising that pays the bills for the Web site).

So how do trip-planning Web sites work? All are simple to use. You go to the Web site and:

- type in your street address, city, state, and zip code
- then type in the same information for your destination
- click the calculate button

After a few seconds, depending on the speed of your modem, a detailed map will appear with directions. Some of these sites also offer directions for getting home.

Along with travel maps, there are links to other Web sites for practically all of your travel needs: hotels and motels; car rental rates; events in the local area; and more. But be aware that a free mapping Web site is often a front door to on-line travel merchants, so the information may not be impartial or complete. Often, Web sites have partnerships with specific car rental companies, hotel chains, and restaurants.

For planning a trip, consult the following Web sites:

www.mapblast.com

www.mapquest.com

www.expediamaps.com

MapBlast

MapBlast (**www.mapblast.com**) gives step-by-step directions, even for major roads and highways, and an estimated amount of time a trip should take (these are extremely optimistic—it's best to add time for traffic, construction, and rest and refueling breaks). You can also get step-by-step maps, a map on how to get home, and with a nifty hot-air balloon icon, you can zoom in on your map.

You can E-mail the map and directions to friends and family for parties or family reunions. When you print, you get a choice of full color, grayscale, and black and white. There are links to other services, such as where to find a nearby Hilton hotel, as well as Web sites for ski vacations, bed-and-breakfasts, car rentals, scheduled events, and live traffic reports.

Web sites cont'd.

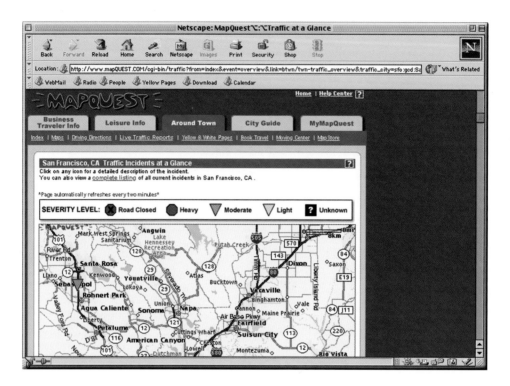

MapQuest

MapQuest (**www.mapquest.com**) has a lot to offer anyone planning a trip (although it's not as easy to use as MapBlast). Not only can you find directions for your next trip, there's a section for live traffic reports for more than 35 U.S. cities—perfect for people who take their laptops on the road with them. There's also mapping based on area codes and telephone exchanges in the U.S. and postal-code mapping for Great Britain. The Travel Guide has information about lodging, food, city info, and weather reports that help you decide whether or not to take a jacket. If you're interested in a Global Positioning System (GPS) for your laptop and car, there is a link to the EarthMate GPS Receiver.

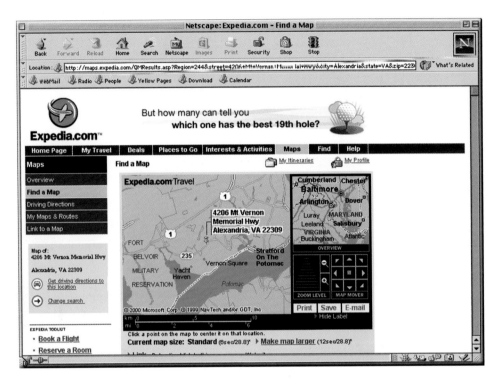

ExpediaMaps

ExpediaMaps (**www.expediamaps.com**) from Microsoft, the software giant, is a Web site with maps for free. In order to take advantage of the site, you have to register your name and provide an E-mail address. It only takes a minute. One thing to note: When you enter your name, you cannot have any spaces, so use an underscore (press the Shift key and then the hyphen key above the letter P on your keyboard. Example: Jane_Smith). When choosing your map, you can select among Shortest, Quickest, and Scenic. ExpediaMaps has a few quirks: You have to enter abbreviations for streets, roads, and drives for best results, such as "Main St." instead of the complete "Main Street." Although ExpediaMaps offers much of the same information as MapQuest and MapBlast, ExpediaMaps is really an on-line advertisement for the retail software version, Microsoft Expedia Streets & Trips 2000.

your on-line travel agent

Book a flight, rental car, and hotel room from your Web browser

The Web can put you in control of planning a trip.

On-line trip-planning services present you with numerous flight options, tell you multiple hotels near your destination, and give a full list of car rental companies at your destination airport (or downtown if you prefer). And these sites are open for business whenever wanderlust strikes.

Want to see how much it would cost to stop off and see Aunt Edna in Chicago? Try out as many options as you like. If prices look too high now, you can save the itinerary and come back in a few weeks when the airlines are having a price war.

Heads up: Each of these sites requires that you register before accessing information. They also request credit card information that will be used to bill tickets and make reservations. But the benefits are enormous, even if you are just an armchair traveler.

Some popular e-Travel sites:

www.expedia.com Doing research on a possible trip? Visit Microsoft's travel Web site and check out dates for different departures and returns. The site saves several itineraries, so you can consult with spouse, family, or friends before committing to a particular trip.

www.travelocity.com Helps you find a plane trip to match your most important criteria. Willing to trade an extra stop for a lower fare? Just tell it that price is more important than a nonstop flight.

www.biztravel.com Business travel is different from personal travel. For one thing, schedule convenience outweighs price in most situations. Among other benefits of biztravel.com, you can keep track of the frequent-flier mileage for multiple airlines.

www.priceline.com Finally, you get some control over flight costs and hotel room rates. Priceline lets you set a price you'd pay, and companies tell you whether they're willing to meet your price. It's a great way to get a cheap, last-minute ticket for a weekend visit to a major U.S. city.

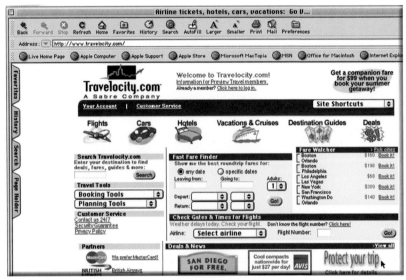

Trying to keep next summer's vacation affordable? Travel sites like Expedia.com help you plan in advance and search for an indirect flight to cut costs.

SK THE EXPERTS

Does it matter which site I use?

Personal preference will ultimately decide which location you select to make travel reservations. Each interface has its quirks, but all of these Web sites tend to tap into common databases of flight information.

Why can't I find bigger discounts?

Some budget airlines and hotels don't show up in on-line travel agency databases. You may have to go directly to the budget company's Web site or poke around for on-line bargains at such sites as **www.cheaptickets.com**.

155

city guides

Find out what's going on in the towns you'll be visiting

Few things are as demoralizing as arriving in a distant city that you've heard is full of excitement and not knowing what to do. Except possibly returning someplace you used to live only to learn that all your old haunts are gone. Thanks to city guides on the Web, you can find out what movie, concert, or museum exhibit is currently showing in almost every town in the country.

Not surprisingly, major cities have some of the most extensive coverage. The two best locations for getting the scoop on big cities are the CitySearch and DigitalCities services (more detail, but only on major cities) and Yahoo!'s Metro Guides (less data, but more cities). Each of these sites can link you to a screening of the latest Hollywood epic and a good place for a quick bite to eat afterward.

For the larger cities, several sites compete with Yahoo!, CitySearch, and DigitalCities to provide information. One good source is generally the local newspaper, which often has its own area guide such as *The New York Times*'s **www.nytoday.com**. The Web sites of alternative newspapers, such as the *San Francisco Bay Guardian*, are another source of what's going on in big towns.

City guides steer you to the happenings in your hometown or places you plan on visiting for business or pleasure.

restaurant guides

On-line restaurant guides serve up the reviews.
They also help steer you to a memorable meal by letting you sort locations by cuisine, neighborhood, or price range. They'll also tell you when reservations are a must, so you can call in advance to ensure you taste the feast that you desire. Although there are numerous regional gastronomic guides, three of the best national directories are:

www.zagat.com The on-line version of the Zagat guides are as opinionated as the original little books that now cover most major metropolitan areas. That's because the same reviews fill both the printed guides and this Web site. You don't have to pay for the on-line version, but you do have to fill out a free registration.

www.cuisinenet.com With coverage of just 16 major U.S. cities, CuisineNet does not have broad coverage. Turn here to get a second opinion on a restaurant that sounded promising at Zagat. Lets you quickly sort by cuisine or neighborhood to track down a best bet.

www.dine.com A major advantage of the reviews on this site is that you can see how different reviewers rated various restaurants. You get to judge the judgers. If they seem to have well-founded reasons for going to one restaurant and avoiding another, you can check out their recommendations for the best places to eat. One drawback to Dine.com: Although it claims to review 125,000 restaurants, the site's coverage lacks strength in the Northeast outside of Boston. Still, it's a great source of information on what types of restaurants exist in smaller towns across the U.S.

international guides

Spending time on the Web helps you look like a local

Just as every country has its own customs, heritage, and language, so every international traveler has individual preferences. Whether you prefer hauling your backpack between hostels or camping out at a local Hilton, you should head to the Web before making major decisions about an international holiday.

Reading through the on-line version of guides works best in planning a trip. Plan on bringing a guidebook with you in case you choose to rearrange your itinerary halfway through the trip. The on-line guides can help you decide which guidebook to purchase.

Here are three sites you can surf on-line for top-flight international information:

www.lonelyplanet.com For tracking down details about out-of-the-way locales or traditional tourist destinations, the Lonely Planet series has gained growing admiration. Some may be put off by the overtly leftish political viewpoints, but the site provides plenty of useful information along with the sermons.

www.fodors.com The "dad" of the on-line travel guides doesn't cover as many locations for free (or with half the attitude) as its younger competitors, but Fodor's allows you to create a custom guide from the elements of its best-selling series. Only interested in hotels in a particular district of Stockholm? Fodor's can paste together a tailored Web page that includes only the information you request or lets you browse through the entire archive of more than 100 cities worldwide.

www.roughguides.com A little cheekier than either of its on-line competitors, the Rough Guides exude the self-confidence of the 20-something crowd to which the British guidebooks cater. The on-line destination guides come straight from the book series and win you over with detailed history about each of the countries, cities, and regions profiled.

 # WHAT IF

You need to know visa restrictions for various countries?

All of the on-line guides tell you whether or not you need to acquire a visa from a country's embassy or consulate. Most foreign governments also have tourist bureaus on the Web that can help you find out where to write for a visa.

You need to learn a country's language before visiting it?

Apple lists the language education products available for the Macintosh at **http://guide.apple.com/uscategories/language_us. html**. You'll find information on software programs that take advantage of your iMac's multimedia capabilities to teach you a language.

CITIZEN ALERT

When you travel overseas, it's always a good idea to keep an eye on the international news. The U.S. State Department tracks riots and epidemics all over the globe. You can view its up-to-date alerts about traveling to specific countries at **www.state.gov** by clicking on the Services icon and linking to Travel Warnings.

FIRST PERSON DISASTER

Listen Up

I hadn't done anything fancy with our computer except E-mail friends and family. Then a friend told me there was a Web site that could help me plan a trip my wife and I were taking to France. There was even a feature that would teach you everyday expressions. I found the site and sure enough it had tons of useful information. Then I clicked on Everyday Expressions in French. The words were there but no sound. I figured I needed speakers so I went to our local computer store and got audio speakers and set them up. I clicked on the Web site. Still no sound. When we went to France, I tried using my newfound French. But when I asked at a newstand to buy a magazine, I got yelled at. When I told our hotel manager about it, he corrected my pronunciation. In French, the words for store and magazine are very similar, but pronounced differently. I was asking to buy the store, instead of a magazine. A week after we were home, my wife asked why I had gotten new speakers for the computer when the built-in ones worked just fine. Oh, and by the way, did I know she had turned off the sound because she didn't like the beeps it made? I quietly asked her how to turn the sound back on.

Anthony S., Sarasota, Florida

now what do I do?

Answers to common problems

Why isn't the Web site responding to my request for a map?

The Internet sometimes suffers data traffic jams that can delay a map site's ability to produce a map for you. If you've been waiting a few minutes, click on your browser's Refresh button. If that doesn't work, there could be a problem with the site or your connection to the Internet. First try another map site to see if it can give you the maps you need. If that fails too, log off from the Internet and log back on after a few minutes. You may find that the delay will disappear when you're back on-line.

Is it safe to purchase my plane tickets over the Web?

Travel was one of the first areas to benefit from on-line purchasing, so travel merchants have a lot of experience making sure your information is secure. Services like Expedia and Travelocity are among the safest places to buy something on the Web.

What is an e-ticket?

Thanks to computers, airlines don't need to send you a paper ticket so you can board your flight. When you request an e-ticket, the airline sends a note reminding you of the purchase. Show the credit card you used for the purchase at the ticket counter (along with your driver's license) and they'll give you your boarding pass.

Where should I look if the major city guides don't cover my destination?

Turn to the search engines. Categorized lists like Yahoo! and Excite work best for finding information on specific locations. Click on Yahoo!'s Regions heading and surf your way from country to state (or province) to local city/town in three clicks.

What if I want to go camping?

The Web contains a wealth of information about parks and regions. The National Park Service details all the national parks at its site (**www.nps.gov**). Most state and local parks departments include similar information about the preserves that they oversee. If you already know what region you'll be visiting, you can guide yourself from state to local areas in Yahoo! (look under the Regional heading for the U.S. States link). They'll help you find towns where you can stock up on groceries (or spend a night before heading out) near the parks you'll be visiting.

Why isn't the travel Web site in English?

Just about every destination attracts native-speaking tourists, but they also want to attract foreigners (that's you), so they produce two versions of the site. Look for an American or British flag. Click on it, and you'll find the English version of the tourist information you're after.

HELPFUL RESOURCES

CONTACTS	BOOKS
Delorme www.delorme.com 1-800-452-5931	**Packing: Bags to Trunks (Chic Simple Components)** By Kim Johnson Gross, Jeff Stone, Walter Thomas
Fodor's www.fodors.com 1-800-733-3000	**Trouble-Free Travel: ...and What to Do When Things Go Wrong** By Stephen D. Colwell and Ann R. Shulman
Lonely Planet www.lonelyplanet.com 1-800-275-8555	**Lonely Planet Travel With Children** By Maureen Wheeler
Rough Guides www.roughguides.com 1-800-526-0275	**The Penny Pincher's Passport to Luxury Travel** By Joel L. Widzer

Games

9

Your iMac is an instant party waiting to happen. In this chapter there are Web sites where you can play games, to say nothing of the many fabulous computer games you can buy. Fun for kids from 1 to 92.

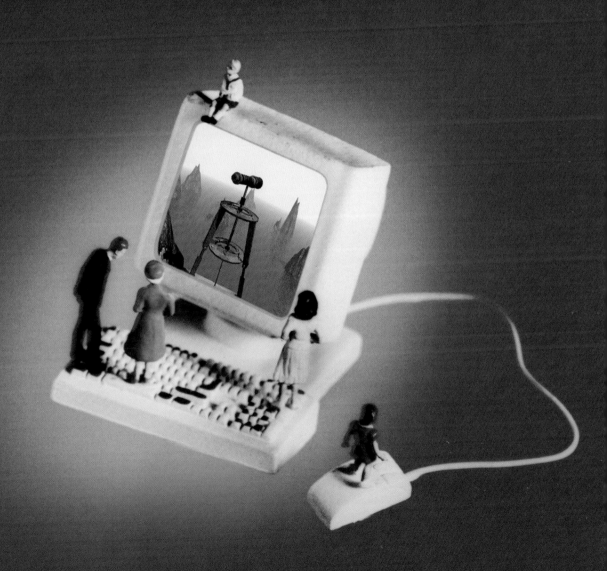

fun software

All work and no play makes Jack a dull boy

Your iMac is the perfect tool to amuse yourself. There are hundreds of Macintosh entertainment software titles that will please all ages. Some re-create traditional board and card games. Others let you fly a plane, teach your children how to read and count, or let you become an all-powerful empire builder intent on total world domination. You can play against a competitor or, when no one's handy, play games like chess or hearts against the computer.

Monday morning quarterbacks can get their football fill all week long with Madden NFL 2000. You choose the teams, the stadium, and the plays. The computer generates the crowd noise and the thumps as bodies collide on-screen.

Pilots talk about the soothing effect of being above the clouds. Why not join them? The flight simulator F/A-18 Hornet shows you what it's like to blast into the wild blue yonder aboard one of the Air Force's fastest jets and shoot down enemy planes. Aviation history buffs should try Flying Circus, which lets you fly a World War I Sopwith Camel.

That's a peach! Swing a virtual club on Links LS and listen to the birds chirping in the trees lining the fairway as your shot sails into the woods.

164

With your iMac playing as your opponent, Hasbro's Mac version of Monopoly shows the dice tumbling and automatically advances its top hat or racing car. Sierra includes several games in its Hoyle collection. You'll know some of the names (such as Crazy Eights), but may not recognize the knockoff of Scrabble, for instance, that goes by the name Double Cross. You can also find several versions of chess on-line, including the freeware MacChess.

SK THE EXPERTS

Do I need another keyboard to play against someone else?

No. If the game allows you to play against someone, the software will let you alternate turns at the keyboard, just like a pinball machine.

What's a joystick?

A joystick adds an arcade feel to your iMac. For example, instead of steering your flight-simulated jet with your mouse, you use the joystick to get a finer feeling of control. You can purchase one at most computer stores.

FIRST PERSON DISASTER

This Window Closed

I was starting to feel pretty good at using my iMac. I could E-mail and surf the Web. Then I saw this software package at the computer store. It was a flight simulator program. I couldn't wait to try it. When I got home, I opened the package and loaded the CD-ROM into my iMac. The software's icon appeared on my desktop and I double-clicked on it. A window appeared with lots of files in it. I clicked on one, and a warning box came up saying it couldn't be opened because the "application that created it could not be found." What?! I called the computer store and asked them what to do. Turns out I had bought a Windows application software package. Meaning it wouldn't work on an Apple computer. If I had read the system requirements at the bottom of the package, I would have seen it was for PC/Windows only. Naturally, because I had opened the software, I couldn't return it.

Laura W., Dayton, Ohio

cool games

Get ready to be dazzled, challenged, knocked off your block...

Fortunately for us, those computer-game programmers didn't just sit around and make imitations of games you know and love. Oh no, they took the amazing graphic power of the computer and along with its tremendous memory created a whole new generation of games that are astounding.

Take *SimCity*, for example. Maxis of Electronic Arts generated this game more than a decade ago, and it's been a huge favorite ever since. SimCity is a simulation game, but instead of simulating a sport or a board game, it simulates an entire city. You act as a city's founding father and city planner and mayor—and watch as the city evolves over the decades. At the start of the game you pick a location and build anything you want upon it—aqueducts, landscaping, factories, houses, and apartment buildings—by dragging each item into place on your town. Then you wait. *SimCity* will calculate how many people will move to your city, based on the kinds of employment, housing, and education you have provided.

You click to set the time line—maybe five years will pass, and perhaps the population declines. If that happens, your city loses funds from its tax base, and you can't afford to build more roads or bigger schools. (Yes, it does get this realistic!) Sometimes a natural disaster will strike, and then you need to figure out how to save your city infrastructure. Sometimes you'll realize you need better schools to attract more workers to your city. Sometimes your place becomes a ghost town, and you need to start again.

It's heady stuff, but it's so well designed that variations of *SimCity* are used to train people considering a career in government or other public service. And you can even play an early, simple version of the game at **simcity.com**, or just watch other people's cities to get an idea of how the game goes.

166

To build your own city, you click-and-drag various building items from a tool bar to your evolving on-screen city. Beware—your choices will either positively or negatively impact the development of your city as it moves through the time line.

more cool games

Ready to be completely challenged?

Want to try your hand at games that are both beautiful and mind-boggling? Then take a crack at *Myst* and *Riven*, two games from Broderbund that combine strange landscapes, pleasant ambient music, and almost no instructions!

Myst came first, and *Riven* is its sequel. In both, when you pop the CD-ROM into its drive and start up the game, you're looking at a landscape with strange features (Is it on another planet? Is that a spaceship? Some strange building? You simply don't know at the beginning.) You use your mouse to point the way you want to explore. You'll come across artifacts and writing you don't under-stand, but gradually, as you figure it out, they all fall together in a cohesive plot.

Although these are true computer games, you'll need to take some notes to crack the story line. You have to provide the pen, but Broderbund, its software maker, provides plenty of pages in a real notebook they include along with the CD-ROM.

Still don't understand what these games are about? Well, the real fun in both is to figure it out for yourself. You become immersed in the worlds of *Myst*, and if anyone tells you exactly what's going on, you probably won't thank them for it in the long run. So set some time aside—make it a whole weekend—and get lost in one of these games. And when you've figured it out, don't give away the secrets to whoever plays it after you. Just drop the occasional hint, and watch them puzzle it out.

In both **Myst** (top) and **Riven** (bottom), the quest is to find a missing object and uncover the story behind it. To move through the game, click on any item, for example, the telescope, to see what it reveals.

entertainment for kids

Here's why today's child is more computer literate than his parents

Don't be fooled by the video arcades or those loud TV ads. Children's computer games, while they look slick and well-scripted, are actually interactive reasoning games that develop a child's deductive powers. For fun and games—with a little bit of a challenge—there's no shortage of CD-ROM games for preschool through grade school years. All children's game software has an age range printed in big type on the box—generally a spread of three or four years, so you'll know what level to pick.

Humongous Entertainment dominates the cartoon game scene for this age group. Its cartoon characters—Putt-Putt the purple car, Pajama Sam, the boy who thinks he's a superhero, Freddi Fish, and Spy Fox—each star in a series of several games called *Junior Adventures*. Each game works in pretty much the same way. Your child sits and watches a cartoon-style introduction that sets up the plot. Each story has a quest element—in *Putt-Putt Saves the Zoo* you must find lost animals in time for the zoo's grand opening, for example—and your child has to find the way to save the day. To move around the place, they point the mouse toward any side of the screen. If that's a direction you can move, the mouse pointer turns into a big arrow. Click on it, and you direct the action that way. There are plenty of characters and challenges to meet on the way, so players need to keep their eyes open for things that might help. Along the way, you need to click on objects to pick them up—you never know when a purple sea anemone or a mug of cocoa will help you get past an obstacle.

ASK THE EXPERTS

How early should a child start on the computer?

Most experts say age 3, but it depends on your child. Bear in mind, your child needs to have some fine motor-skill development to be able to handle the mouse successfully. The key is to monitor your child's enjoyment of the computer; if she gets frustrated, move on to something else, like a book or a noncomputer game.

I can't afford a CD-ROM game right now. How can I keep everyone entertained on the computer?

There are plenty of Web sites that feature interactive games you can try out for free. Go to Disney's site (**www.disney.com**) and click on the games link there, and you'll find many computer-based activities for children. At Headbone Interactive (**www.headbone.com**) there are lots of games for preteens. Or visit Nickelodeon's site (**www.nickjr.com**) for activities based on favorite characters from Blue's Clues and the Busy World of Richard Scarry. For more on-line games, go to Yahoo! Games (**games.yahoo.com**) and click on any game your child might like.

In *Putt-Putt Saves the Zoo* the cursor turns into a big arrow, so when you click on any part of the screen, that's where Putt-Putt (the little purple car) will go. You can also click on various items, such as a newspaper or oil can, and they will appear in the dashboard to be used to solve problems later in the game.

learning games

For preschoolers there's a host of friendly character-based software. *Reader Rabbit* has one of the more venerable characters in the digital world. He's the star of a series of programs that start teaching the very young (ages 18 months and up) basic computer, math, and language skills—and ends up in school-age titles teaching them third grade math. Knowledge Adventures' *JumpStart Toddlers, JumpStart Preschool,* and *JumpStart Spanish* cover the same territory, with pictures that you click on to visit games, painting, and click-and-drag building activities. For the very young, *Toddlers* greets players with a friendly Giggles the Gopher, a character who points out seven "hot spots" that kids can click on to visit activity areas.

For grade school children the educational titles get a bit more challenging. These software "games" are designed to complement what students are learning in the classroom. The *JumpStart* and *Reader Rabbit* titles—and Humongous Entertainment's *Big Thinkers*, too—provide grade-based general activities. And there are titles geared to specific subjects, to give a boost in areas where a child may be flagging—such as *JumpStart Phonics Learning System* or *Reader Rabbit's Math Ages 6-9*. To get a good overview of appropriate titles, check out the reviews at these sites: **www.kbkids.com** or **www.familypc.com**.

JumpStart Spanish teaches vocabulary by having the child click on an item to both hear and see the Spanish word.

ASK THE EXPERTS

Can my child stop halfway through a program?

It's possible to get through a *Junior Adventure* title in a few hours, but that's too long for a little one to sit still. So you can press your keyboard's S key to save a game (the screen you're at will appear in a little photo album), and when you start the game again, you press L (for load) and click on the scene you just left to go back to where you were. The *Junior Adventures* are very well scripted and funny, so that they can keep even boisterous preteens entertained (though they're aimed at 3- to 10-year-olds).

How do I help my child stay motivated to learn on these computer learning games?

Each of the reading and math titles in the *Reader Rabbit* series features a section where parents can create and print award certificates. These colorful, authentic looking "achievement" certificates will help keep your child motivated to go to the next level. They also make nice wall decorations!

How do I introduce a computer game to a toddler?

The best way for toddlers to pick this up is sitting on your lap, watching as you move the mouse. If you let the little one call the shots, sooner or later you'll find the mouse grabbed out of your hand, and you can leave the tyke to get on with it.

now what do I do?

Answers to common problems

Where can I find reviews of games?

Between on-line game review sites and print publishers' Web archives of past reviews, you should have no problem finding information on a particular title. Two general locations for game reviews are CNET's GameCenter and ZDNet's GameSpot. For specific information on children's games, try the Children's Software Revue (**www.childrenssoftware.com**), Kidsdomain (**www.kidsdomain.com**), or *FamilyPC* magazine (**www.familypc.com**).

How can I tell if a program I see in the store will run on my iMac?

All games have a list of system requirements on the side of their box. If it says that it will run on a Macintosh-based computer, it will almost certainly run on your iMac. Some titles say that they require a "minimum" of processor, operating system, and memory. It's okay if you have a more recent version of the operating system, more memory, or a faster processor. You just can't have less than the game requires. Check your iMac before leaving for the store by clicking on the Apple menu and selecting the Apple System Profiler option. Your iMac will display a window detailing the basic information about its innards. Print it out and take it with you.

What does it mean when the computer keeps saying that the colors need to be set to 256 when I'm trying to play an old computer game?

Like most modern monitors, your iMac's display can show millions of colors. But in the early days of the Macintosh some computers could display only 16 colors—or none at all. Programmers always wanted higher quality, so they occasionally wrote applications that wouldn't run unless there were 256 colors. Unfortunately, they didn't make that "at least 256 colors," so anything with more than 256 colors (like your iMac) has to be reset to the lower number.

Do this by clicking on the Monitor Bit Depth control on the control strip at the bottom of your iMac's screen—it's the one with color bars on the monitor. Some programs will automatically make this adjustment for you. Beware, however, of games that require 16 colors. The minimum number of colors that the iMac can display is 256, and trying to run these lower-resolution games can cause your machine to crash.

Can staring at a computer screen for too long harm children's eyesight?

It's a good idea to limit a toddler's time at a computer to about ten minutes per session, and follow it with activities that don't require them to focus on objects at close range.

How realistic is it to expect my children and their friends to play on the computer together peacefully?

Your computer is only a tool. If your children normally play nicely with their friends, they should be able to do so on the computer. Actually, many educational software titles for children encourage them to yell out answers, sing along, and play games with the characters on the screen. All of this can be done with more than one person playing the game at the same time.

ELPFUL RESOURCES

CONTACTS

Pangea Software, Inc. (Bugdom)
www.pangeasoft.net
1-512-266-9991

Microsoft (Links LS)
www.microsoft.com/games
1-425-882-8080

Aspyr Media, Inc. (Madden)
www.aspyr.com
1-512-708-8100

Graphic Simulations Corp. (F/A 18)
www.graphsim.com
1-972-386-7575

Hasbro (Monopoly)
www.hasbro.com
1-800-400-1352

Sierra On-Line Inc.
www.sierra.com
1-425-649-9800

Knowledge Adventures
www.knowledgeadventure.com
1-310-793-0600

Humongous Entertainment
www.humongous.com
1-800-499-8386

Electronic Arts (SimCity)
www.simcity.com
1-800-245-4525

Red Orb (Myst)
www.redorb.com
1-415-895-2000

BOOKS

The Macintosh Bible Guide to Games
By Bart Farkas

glossary

Active window Even when you have lots of different windows open, you can work on only one at a time. It's called the active window, and you can tell which it is by looking at the title bar—on the active window, it will be brightly colored, and the others will be fainter. Also, the active window will be in front of all the others.

Arrow key On a keyboard, there are four arrow keys to the right of the letters. They point up, down, left, and right, and are used to move the cursor inside a window.

Balloons Helpful callouts that tell you the role of each item on your computer. They're called balloons because they're the same shape as dialog balloons in cartoons.

Apple key On either side of your keyboard's spacebar are two Apple keys, which you can identify by Apple Computer's distinctive logo of an apple with a bite taken out of it. The Apple key can also be used in combination with other keys such as the letter "s" to save a file, the letter "o" to open a file, the letter "x" to cut, and the letter "v" to paste.

Apple Menu The menu that contains the essential features of the Macintosh operating system. Click on the Apple icon on the upper left of your screen and you'll see the Apple menu.

Application Menu The menu on the upper right of your screen that contains a list of all applications or software programs that are currently running on your computer. The active application is listed under Finder when you start your computer.

Bit A bit is the smallest amount of information a computer can handle. You'll see it used most often to describe the depth or quality of information, such as 24-bit color, 16-bit sound, and so on. The higher the number you see, the better the quality—and the larger the size of the files!

Browser A program used to view (and hear) the information on the World Wide Web.

Byte A byte is the basic unit of storage on your computer. It's made up of 8 bits, and it's so small that most of the files you'll see are measured in thousands of bytes (kilobytes, or KB) or millions of bytes (megabytes or MB). Most hard disks these days can hold thousands of millions of bytes, or gigabytes (GB).

CD-ROM They look like music CDs, but CD-ROMs contain computer data, not just audio tracks.

Chat On a computer, chat doesn't involve your voice at all. It's a typed live conversation between two or more people, all of whom are on-line at the same time. Chats can take place in chat room sites or by using a program like AOL's Instant Messenger or AIM.

Chooser The part of the Macintosh system that lets you choose your printer. You find Chooser listed under the Apple menu.

Clipboard An out-of-the-way place where your iMac puts the last item that you cut—whether text, graphics, or sounds. To view what's currently in the Clipboard, select the View Clipboard option on the Finder's View menu.

Click With an iMac, you click once to select an item (whether a file or a window). You click twice to open a file, display the contents of a folder, or launch an application.

Close box One of the four boxes that help you command a window. Click on a window's Close box and it will (surprise!) close.

Collapse box The second of the four window boxes for arranging a window. The Collapse box shrinks a window to its Title bar.

Control key At the far left of your keyboard is the Control key. Like the Apple and Option keys, the Control key can also be used in combination with other keys to provide shortcut features on your iMac.

Control Panels The place where you adjust certain features in your iMac, such as the Time and Date feature. You can open individual controls by selecting the Control Panel option from the Apple menu.

Control Strip The bar with several icons that runs across the bottom of your screen. The Control Strip provides one-click access to certain controls on the Control Panels.

Cursor Moving the mouse on your desk surface moves a little picture on your computer screen. That picture is the cursor. It usually looks like an arrow, but sometimes it's shaped like an hourglass or the letter I.

Cut A Macintosh feature that lets you remove an item from one place and put it on the Clipboard so you can paste it someplace else.

Digital Everything that goes on in your computer is digital—it's a code made up of long strings of digits (0s or 1s), unlike telephone or radio signals, which are made up of lots of different frequencies.

Desk Accessory Mini-applications such as the Macintosh calculator that make your iMac more useful.

Desktop The Desktop is everything you see on the screen before you open any programs or folders. It consists of the Macintosh Hard Drive and other icons.

Dialogue box Another name for a window that asks you to click on a button or enter a word is a dialogue box. It's called that because your iMac wants you to respond in some way—like two people talking.

Disk (floppy) Also called diskettes, floppy disks are the 3 1/2 inch square things that people once slipped in and out of their Macintoshes. Being square and hard, they don't look like floppy disks—but underneath that plastic casing, there are circles made of flexible mylar. If someone offers you a file on a floppy, ask them to E-mail it instead. Your iMac doesn't have a floppy drive to read it.

Disk (hard) All the programs and files on your computer are stored on a hard disk, also called a hard drive. These are circles of metal in a hard casing stored inside your computer.

Drag To hold down the mouse button and move the mouse. Used to move highlighted text or move files in and out of folders.

E-Mail Typed messages that are delivered from one computer to another over the Internet.

Extensions The innards of your iMac's system software reside in the Extensions Manager. If you accidentally open Extensions Manager, close it. Only make changes to an extension if you're directed to do so by technical support—or unless you really know what you're up to. Changing an extension can harm the performance of your iMac.

File All the information you see on a computer, and all the programs you run, are stored in files.

File format Different types of information (text, pictures, or sounds) are stored or formatted in files in different ways. This is called the file format. Usually, the icon next to the file gives you a clue as to its format. In Appleworks, a text file has a icon with an A on it, while a graphics file has an icon with a pencil.

Finder Effectively, this is the Macintosh operating system. Finder lets you "find" files or applications by hunting through folders.

Folder In your iMac as in a regular office, files are stored in folders. Using Finder, you'll see little manila folder icons tucked away in most drives. Double-click on them, and they will open up to reveal the files inside.

Font The style and size of the type is called the font. In a word processor, you'll see font names like Times New Roman or Ariel, and font sizes such as 10 point or 12 point. There are also font styles like Bold and Italic.

Icon Little pictures appear frequently on your iMac. The ones that do something when you click on them are called icons because they are pictures that represent an action or file.

Internet A massive network of computers that stretches across the entire world.

Menu At the top of almost every Macintosh program are words like File, Edit, and Help. These are menu headings. Click on them and a menu pops down with choices, such as Open, Save, and Quit.

Option key To the left of your keyboard's spacebar is the Option key. Like the Apple and Control keys, the Option key can also be used in combination with other keys as a shortcut to certain features.

Paste The action that lets you place in your document whatever you've Cut or Copied.

QuickTime Apple's application for displaying images and videos on your iMac.

Reset button Most iMacs have a reset button located on its right side. Push it to restart your iMac if it "crashes"—suddenly stops working.

Restart A menu option on the Special menu that lets you restart your iMac. Many applications request that you restart your computer after you install software.

Sad Mac If a picture of a small computer appears with a frown on its face when you first start your iMac, you've got a Sad Mac. It means something is wrong with your iMac. Call whomever sold you your computer and ask where to go for technical help.

Scroll bar Allows you to move a window's contents up and down or side to side.

Sherlock Your iMac's special search feature that lets you find an item on your hard drive or the Internet.

Shut down The menu option on the Special menu that turns off your iMac.

Size box The third of the four boxes that help you manipulate a window. The size box is at the bottom right of every Window and lets you adjust a window's size to suit your viewing.

Sleep The menu option on the Special menu that turns your iMac into a sleeping beauty. When you touch the mouse button or a keyboard key, your iMac will wake up.

Smiley Mac The Happy Computer icon that normally greets you when you start your iMac and lets you know everything is OK.

Title bar The title bar is the top part of a window. It contains the name of that window's folder or program.

URL (Uniform Resource Locator) Techspeak for an Internet address.

Web (a.k.a. World Wide Web) The Web is part of the Internet that contains almost all the sites, sounds, and pictures that you want to visit.

Window The place where you see the contents of a folder or file.

Zoom box The final box that allows you to adjust a window. The Zoom box lets you instantly increase the size of a window to reveal all its contents without having to play with its size.

index

Page numbers in italics refer to illustrations.

H

hackers, 61, 117, 130
hard drive (HD), 22, 25
Hasbro, 165, 175
Headbone Interactive, 171
Heartland Family Graphics, 143
help
    Adobe, 113
    America Online (AOL), 95
    Apple Computer Corp., 33, 113
    AppleWorks, 39, 53
    Aspyr Media, Inc., 175
    Block Financial Corp., 131
    Corel, 53
    Delorme, 161
    Earthlink, 81
    Electronic Arts, 175
    Fodor's, 161
    Graphic Simulations Corp., 175
    Hasbro, 175
    Humongous
        Entertainment, 175
    Intuit, 131
    Knowledge Adventures, 175
    Learning Company, The, 113
    Leister Productions, Inc., 145
    Links LS, 175
    Lonely Planet, 161
    Macsense Connectivity, 33
    Microsoft, 53, 81, 95
    Netscape, 95
    Pangea Software, 175
    Red Orb, 175
    Reunion, 145
    Rough Guides, 161
    setting up your iMac, 8
    Sierra, 175
highlighting text, 42

Home, 68
HotBot, 81
HotMail, 85
house, finding on-line, 125
How to Trace Your Family Tree: A Complete and Easy to Understand Guide for the Beginner (American Genealogical Research Institute), 145
Hoyle collections of games, 165
http, 71
Humongous Entertainment, 170, 172, 175
hyperlink. *See* link
Hypertext Transfer Protocol, 71

I

I-beam, 36, 42
icons, 18
    changing color, 21
    defined, 21
iMac, 9, *10*
    connecting your modem, *58*
    logging on, 16–17
    plugging in, 10–11, *11*
    setting up, 8–9
    turning off, 30–31, *32*
    turning on, *14*, 14–15
    unpacking, 9
indenting text, 46, 47
information superhighway.
        See Internet
InfoSeek, 81
Instant Messenger, 77–78
instruction book, 10
international guides, 158
Internet, 54–81

M

Mac Answers!: Certified Tech Support (Levitus and Brisbin), 33

MacChess, 165

MacInTax, 126, *126*, 127

Macintosh Bible, The (Aker), 33

Macintosh Bible Guide to Games, The (Farkas), 175

Macsense Connectivity, 33

Make Alias, 37

MapBlast, 151

mapping software, 148

MapQuest, 152

margins, 46, *47*

Marx, Dave, 95

Microsoft, 153
  help, 53, 81, 95

Microsoft Network (MSN), 60

Microsoft Word, 36, 37

.mil, 71

Minimize box, 23

modems, 58
  connecting, 58, *58*
  speed, 58

monitor
  256 colors, 174
  Monitor Bit Depth control, 174

Monopoly, 165

Morningstar, 119

Morris, Kenneth M., 131

Morris, Virginia B., 131

mortgage, shopping on-line for, 124–125

Motley Fool, 119

mouse, 9, 14, *20*, 20–21
  cleaning, 33

mouse pad, 20

mouse pointer, 20
  jumping, 33

My Files folder, 44

Myst, 168, *169*

N

National Park Service, 161

Navigator, *66*, 67, 71

.net, 71

Netscape
  help, 95
  Navigator, *66*, 67, 71
  new message alert, 88

New York Times, The, 156

Nickelodeon, 171

9 Steps to Financial Freedom, The (Orman), 131

Non-Designer's Design Book, The: Design and Typographic Principles for the Visual Novice (Williams), 113

Northern Light, 81

O

on-line checks, stopping, 123

On-line services, 56, 60, 64, 84
  compared to ISPs, 65

Opera, 67

operating system, 14, 24

Optical Character Recognition (OCR), 109

.org, 71

Orman, Suze, 131

Outlook Express, *88, 93*
  address book, 92, 93
  new message alert, 88, 94

THE AUTHOR: UP CLOSE

Chris Sandlund, an accomplished technology writer, spent seven years learning the workings of the computer business in Silicon Valley. He returned to the East Coast in 1987 to work as an editor at *Home Office Computing*. He has also written for *PC/Computing*, *Small Business Computing*, and *FamilyPC*. Because he serves as unofficial technical support for the entire Sandlund clan, he knows the pain and suffering involved in using computers. He wrote *I'm Turning on My iMac, Now What?!*™ with their needs in mind.